By Andy Begley

I didn't row the Atlantic
#so*what*

"You don't need to have rowed the Atlantic to have valuable life skills to share. Andy is in an incredibly informed position to advocate and share experiences across a wide range of specialisms. I've been round the world 11 times and think I know what it means to travel, but I don't pretend to be a motivational speaker offering leadership advice. We do have one thing in common though, I think . . . the capacity for self-examination and ability to look at life through a different lens."

Nick Sanders MBE – world record-holding adventurer and author who has circumnavigated the world on both bicycles and motorbikes

CONTENTS

Chapter 1	There's a queue at Everest, FFS	13
Chapter 2	The obvious is an antidote to curiosity	19
Chapter 3	Pareto, Dilbert, and perceptions of wisdom	26
Chapter 4	The sun will still rise if the cockerel doesn't crow	32
Chapter 5	Custodians of culture . . . and rule number seven	42
Chapter 6	Certainty, uncertainty, discipline & hygiene	51
Chapter 7	B-class c-suites?	59
Chapter 8	Confidence tricks & boardroom aikido	64
Chapter 9	Data is not a f*cking fossil fuel	70
Chapter 10	The benefits of foresight, and the comfort of not knowing	79
Chapter 11	Evolution doesn't have to be competitive	87
Chapter 12	What free words	93
Chapter 13	Pre-mortem for a permacrisis	99
Chapter 14	Success(ion)	106

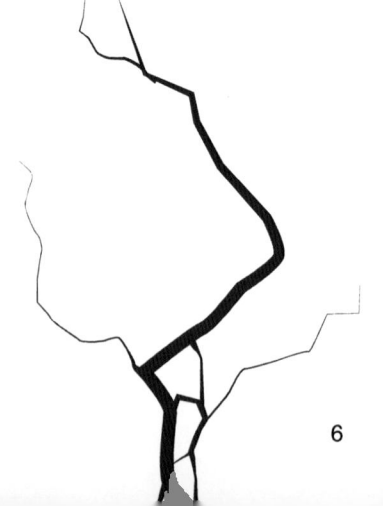

INTRODUCTION

I hate being taught anything, but I do love learning. And in many ways, I feel this is what compels me to write this book.

That might sound like a paradox – in fact this book is full of very intentional paradoxes…but indulge me for just a moment.

Meeting someone who has the ability to teach me something, without preaching or patronising, is a very rare find indeed, and something I value immensely.

I 'learn' in different ways – picking up snippets of wisdom from other industries, sectors and cultures and contemplating how I might be able to apply them in my own corporate world at an unknown juncture somewhere further down the line.

It's impossible to know what's going to be of use to you until that moment arrives. But the more you can tuck away in your memory bank, the better prepared you'll be when it happens.

What makes me qualified to be telling you all this?

After all, I've never attempted to row single-handed across the Atlantic.

I haven't scaled the world's tallest peak to plant my flag at the summit of Everest.

And I have no desire whatsoever to brave the elements on a trek to the North or South Pole.

You won't find any of my career achievements splashed across the front pages of a national newspaper, captured on YouTube, or smeared over social media either.

And that's just fine by me.

Because I'm a firm believer that it's not about what you do in life, but what you learn along the way . . . and crucially, how you choose to use all of that information.

So why am I putting pen to paper to write this, you might quite reasonably ask?

What makes my opinion any more relevant or revolutionary than the next person?

Maybe nothing. But maybe a lot. In their own way, I believe that everyone has it in them to be a leader; everyone can be a hero. You just need a good selection of tools to ensure you can tackle every challenge that comes your way.

I am driven by frustration, not ego.

In a frank, honest and well-reasoned way, I want to share the tools and strategies that have helped me on my own career journey, the crossroads I have reached when I've had to be brave enough to make a choice, and the lightbulb moments which have helped me to appreciate that there are more ways than you might think to solve any given problem.

And if, at the end of all this, the result is something of a 'go-to' companion that provides a resource for innovation, business solutions, and opportunities to look at life's challenges a little bit differently, then I'll consider it a job well done.

So, let me ask you a question: do you find yourself getting frustrated with the menu of bland, tired, traditional and increasingly repetitive management tools and techniques? I do. There are many occasions where I hear my inner voice telling me: "There must be a better way".

The mere fact that a person has risen to the top of an organisation doesn't automatically make them the cleverest kid in town.

You don't have to wait for scraps of wisdom to be thrown down to you from their top table, because there are solutions all around you.

Just because a person is in a leadership position doesn't make them a leader. Never forget that.

You can pay an awful lot of money to be told by so-called 'experts' how complex and multi-faceted successful leadership is, but at its very core, it's really just based on simple ideas and principles, and generous helpings of human decency.

Appreciate and believe that, and you have the ability to change the way you think about everything.

Leaders don't go to chief executive training college, because there's no such thing.

As Buddhist sage Chan Master Fuchan Yuan said: "There are three essentials to leadership: humility, clarity and courage."

Some of the ideas in here are what you might describe as 'common sense' except for one crucial fact: if that was the case, everyone would already be following them, and they're not.

That's what motivates me to put pen to paper.

I'm a huge admirer of talented, driven individuals who have achieved amazing things in their life and now want to share their experiences with the world. But the truth is, there are only so many conferences, masterclasses, speeches, and presentations you can attend before you start to question some of the fundamental messages.

And remember, there's a snaking queue at Everest's base camp these days for those who feel the need to add their footprints in the snow!

I've always been interested in the science of leadership, but increasingly find myself trying to cut through all the chaff. There's a lot of spouting for spouting's sake in the corporate world these days. A lot of vanilla. Theories that are bland, baffling, or too safe.

People have a natural inclination to latch onto what resonates with them; we like listening to like-minded people because they reinforce our own beliefs, and make us feel comforted and reassured.

But that's really dangerous in my opinion. Restrict yourself to this audience and you'll always be trapped in your private thought bubble.

Creating your own echo chamber is really perilous, but it's a trap which is so easy for us to fall into.

I'm not trying to copy anyone with my views in here, or simply reach out to connect with those who will agree with every word I say.

I believe it's incredibly important to recognise the type of people you are automatically attracted to – not always for logical, healthy reasons – to keep this constantly on your radar.

Whenever I'm putting a management team together, avoiding the echo chamber scenario is something I am acutely aware of. I don't want to surround myself with a group of people who will automatically resonate with my way of thinking. Or indeed appoint a procession of 'yes' men and women who lack the courage to challenge my views – or think that I'd object if they did.

That's why it is crucial to create a degree of friction and difference in a very close team. How are you and your organisation ever going to evolve if your senior team constantly aligns with what you already think or do?

Now, more than ever, as we speed through the fourth industrial revolution towards an even more frenetic fifth, taking a risk and trying something different is no longer the most dangerous strategy. Standing still, and settling for the status quo, is far more dangerous.

And yet most people haven't even fully got their heads around the fourth industrial revolution yet . . . so what chance do they stand of appreciating and preparing for the fifth?

I consider myself to be something of a generalist in a specialist world. Over the course of my career, I've worked in hospitality, health and social care, local government, and much more.

I believe this blend of experience, jobs and knowledge gained from roles at all levels has given me something of a unique perspective, and shown me how my managerial tool box is totally transferrable.

I didn't have a career plan, but have always been driven to be the best I can be in any given environment.

Sometimes, I'd be taking in vital knowledge without realising it at the time.

The key is to draw on it, embrace it, appreciate it, and act upon it – even if it is much further down the line. You can't possibly know when you are going to need it.

I've learned some simple, hard truths along the way, and also plenty of less obvious skills or attributes too. Some of these were very subtle nuances which I didn't dwell on at the time – but on reflection I have come to appreciate their importance.

A colleague said to me the other day: "I knew you were a different kind of chief executive, because you actually said hello to me in the car park".

What? That really took me aback. Doesn't everyone do that if they bump into a colleague on the way into the office? Isn't that just a basic example of human decency, regardless of where you might sit in a business hierarchy?

Apparently not, which is a sad – but also dangerous – indictment. I learned this lesson very early in my career, working in the leisure and tourism sector, when people would smile and say hello.

Needless to say, it left a lasting impression, and made me feel that little bit happier and more valued, for the rest of the day.

This was a discipline which was instilled in me at a very early age in one of my earliest jobs, where you could land yourself with a written warning if you were caught without a smile on your face, and didn't say a cheery 'hello' to people you met.

Why should an organisation reprimand you for not smiling and saying good morning to people? Are they right, or fair? I realise now that it taught me some brilliant lessons; we'll elaborate on this later.

At the time I thought this could only really be appropriate in the hospitality or holiday and leisure industry, but have since come to appreciate its power in every single walk of life. It can have a profound impact.

> **People disregard these 'soft skills' as they move up the corporate tree at their peril, for they will repay you many times over and can unlock many a difficult conflict.**

When you're a chief executive though, you're never going to be loved by everyone – however sociable you might be in the car park!

A quarter of your audience won't ever like you. That may be down to the way that you look, the way that you speak, how you walk, or simply the perception of the person you 'must be' because of the position you've come to hold.

In a world where many crave 24/7 love and endorsement on social media, this can be a hard pill to swallow, but you have to get over it.

And one of the ways is to only fight the battles you have a chance of winning in business. Concentrate on the other 75%. Otherwise you're wasting a hell of a lot of effort.

How many of you have been in a scenario where a manager has chosen a course of action simply on the basis that 'we've always done it this way?'

You know what they say: do what you have always done, and you'll get what you've always got. And we're back to the perils of standing still once again.

Traumatic as it was for so many people, the Covid pandemic did at least force us to contemplate fresh ways of doing business. We had to think very differently about things…. about everything.

It opened people's eyes to the fact that there is always more than one way of solving a problem, and compelled us to be innovative, imaginative, and creative.

It catapulted our working practices forward, accelerating the uptake of digital solutions, and super-charging our thinking.

I'm not claiming that I'm breaking new ground with any of this. All the ingredients, methods, clues and cues for success are with us – the key is how you recognise them, and choose to use them.

And how you use yourself too. They say staff are your greatest resource, but in fact it's you who are your greatest resource.

Let's make the most of ourselves. Let's seize the moment, and harness that creativity and innovation, and focus on doing the right things… right now.

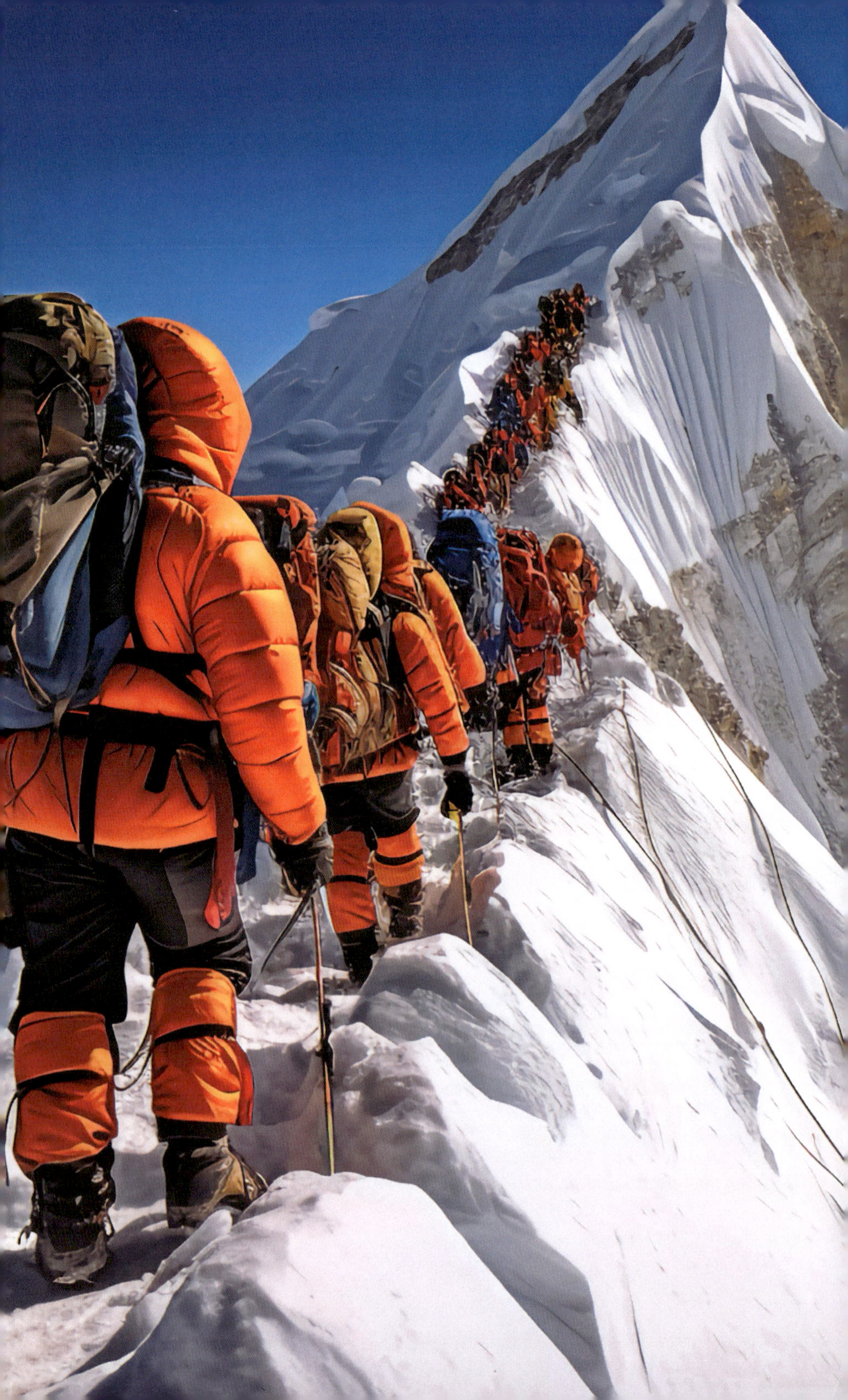

CHAPTER *one*

There's a queue at Everest, FFS

I'm not going to disrespect anyone who has climbed to the top of Mount Everest, because I know for a fact I couldn't bloody well do it.

It remains a hell of an achievement. But I wonder if it ever occurs to all those who queue patiently to plant their flags and footprints at the summit that this is not such a headline-maker as it used to be?

The world is a much smaller and more tech-enabled place these days, making it unquestionably easier for us to pursue our adventures.

At the same time though, these advances in technology have created a platform for people to shout much louder about what they're doing – making it more difficult for us to extract the useful nuggets from the overdose of unwanted and unwarranted noise.

Doing things which get us noticed is one thing, but having the right motivations behind them is quite another.

I've encountered too many people over the years who have conquered their own private Everest for no other reason than just to be able to say they've done it, so they then feel sufficiently qualified to come back and champion themselves as some sort of managerial or motivational guru.

That sticks in my craw. I'm not for a moment demeaning the achievements of true adventurers and boundary-pushing pioneers, just pointing out that there is no automatic correlation with the summit they reach, and the gravitas or value of the person who reaches it.

For the majority of us, going to work and doing the best possible job, or raising a happy and healthy family, is a summit in itself.

And whatever some middle managers seem to think, I know that the overwhelming majority of people go to work determined to do a really good job. They are enthused, energised, committed, incentivised, and proud.

Today more than ever, it's not just the salary that motivates workers. Ask the modern generation of Gen Z and Gen Alpha what qualities they look for in an employer and they'll tell you they are just as focused on a moral contract, where they can align their behaviours and beliefs with the corporate social responsibility policies of the organisation they work for.

They're also more likely to choose a portfolio career which doesn't involve working nine-to-five for one single employer, for years upon end.

And that's all great, because it reshapes the employment market, and challenges the way in which organisations have got to learn how to function . . . for the better.

This is in stark contrast to our education system, which although operating in the 21st century, is still very much embedded in increasingly detached Victorian values.

What comes out of this is often a very restricted way of thinking, and a traditional, dated framework which carries through into a world of employment where life is evolving at a significant rate.

That doesn't strike me as being particularly compatible, or indeed sustainable. We need to ensure that we are liberating some of the talent and thinking which could sadly find itself being constrained in these age-old structures.

I believe that most people are far more invested in their jobs these days than any job description, person spec, or contract of employment can ever truly convey.

Most people put far more into their job than any piece of paper can hope to portray.

Yet many organisations still try to hold committed and hard-working people to account against their contractual small print, which strikes me as slightly perverse. I believe it's a motivational contraceptive, and is a guaranteed recipe for sub-optimal results.

If you want to truly get into new world ideas to address new world problems, then you have got to ensure your framework does not find itself stubbornly stuck in a rut.

And we must never fall into the trap of just focusing on those people who grab the spotlight and mercilessly exploit social media platforms to talk up their headlines.

In my experience, it's usually those who are just getting on with doing a good job rather than spending too much time shouting about it, who are the real hidden gems.

For me, it's not simply about what anyone has achieved, or indeed what their motivations were for achieving it, but how they then use the wisdom and knowledge they have gained for game-changing purposes.

Not everyone who has queued to reach the Everest summit will fit into this mould Many did it simply so they could tell people they were there, and grab a selfie as they planted a flag in the ground. They have nothing more to offer than a hollow boast.

If their quest was driven by a motivation to better themselves on the other hand, broaden their thinking, or arm themselves with new and valuable life skills which gifted them with a fresh and alternative perspective on life, it's a different matter altogether.

I suppose what I'm really saying here is that some people's 'adventures' are more contrived than others.

If you're lucky enough to have the financial clout to set off on a global expedition, or can garner the sort of sponsorship you need to back you, then good for you. There's absolutely nothing wrong with that.

But these people are often driven by the thought that they can make a good living off the back of their travels – and that's very different to those who are following a raw passion, seeking to achieve something that is of great emotional importance. These people have far more credibility. The key, of course, is being able to tell the difference.

There's a Nepalese mountaineer called Nirmal Purja, known as 'Nims', who holds countless world records and is overflowing with motivational credibility.

Prior to taking on a career in mountaineering, he served in the British Army with the Brigade of Gurkhas, followed by the Special Boat Service – the special forces unit of the Royal Navy. When it comes to gathering and sharing incredible life experiences, he is the real deal.

He is a man who demonstrates that with the right mindset, planning and team, all things are possible. He has been inspiring people of all ages, showing how a positive approach can lead to the most incredible achievements in life.

As explorer and author Reinhold Messner says, Nims has a great capacity for economic management, leadership, logistics organisation, and obviously, exceptional physical resistance.

There is a fabulous Netflix documentary called 14 Peaks which is worth checking out. It illustrates the sheer determination and willpower of Nims to make the impossible possible, and is filled with motivational quotes which are relevant to any walk of life. For example:

- *"Don't be afraid to dream big. It doesn't matter where you come from."*
- *"I was told that my project was impossible, so I decided to make it Project Possible. You can show the world that nothing is impossible."*
- *"I have to compete against myself to be better than who I was yesterday."*
- *"Sometimes when you feel like you are completely f*cked, you are actually only 45% f*cked."*

It's brilliant. When you are feeling exhausted, you've always got more in your tank than you think.

Nims also spoke about the importance of being willing to try, and appreciating that this means, on the flipside, there is always a chance you may fail.

It's an important reminder that sometimes in life, you have got to take risks if you are going to make big things happen for yourself.

This is what I'm talking about. That's what I call a motivational role model. Nims is a walking example that everything in life is possible, even if you're armed only with a determined approach and positive mindset.

He's far more than just a social media photoshoot opportunity at the summit. As I say, it's vital when you're hunting around for role models to be able to separate the wheat from the chaff.

Understanding people's motivations for whatever they do in life is key to this. And whether they're the highest climber, fastest driver, or deepest diver, there's always a way to make a direct link from these people's exploits back to the challenges we all face in our own lives and workplaces.

> **It's the value base of an individual that interests me; what drives an individual's behaviour, what drives corporate behaviour too – and understanding where that drive is coming from.**

I'm talking here about behavioural economics, using a degree of psychology to understand how and why people behave the way they do in the real world. We'll be talking a lot about this over the course of the coming chapters.

This is closely linked to a person's value base . . . how much do they perceive they are worth, and what is the basis of this opinion? The best and most successful managers are tuned into this.

Challenging your thinking around colleagues, and trying to understand their value base, will make it far easier for you to communicate with people in a way which stimulates them, around issues they consider to be important.

There are Pioneers in life, there are Prospectors, and there are Settlers. Chris Rose covers this issue well in the book 'What Makes People Tick'.

Broadly speaking, a Pioneer is someone who is motivated by the idea of self-realisation; fulfilling their own potential. They are driven by displays of fairness, and the principle that, to quote that well-known Vulcan scholar, Star Trek's Mr Spock: "The needs of the many outweigh the needs of the few."

Pioneers are ambitious, but they seek personal fulfilment and contentment, rather than chasing the plaudits of others. They have their own internal moral compass.

Prospectors, on the other hand, are driven by receiving the esteem of others. They're the ones who will always be first to post/boast about their achievements on social media, and are most likely to lie awake at night worried about how many 'likes' or 'shares' they're getting.

Prospectors are motivated by success, status, and levels of recognition, and are far more conscious of the importance of image. Style over substance, perhaps? That's a whole other talking point.

Then there are Settlers who some people feel will always tend to be an older age demographic than Prospectors. I actually don't think that's true.

Settlers will have a more glass-half-empty perspective on life, and be more worried about the immediate issues impacting themselves and their families, rather than looking too far ahead at the bigger picture. They're motivated far more by solutions to perceived threats, and the efficient ticking of security boxes.

What's interesting here is that you think these groups would be divided up on the basis of socio-economic status, and/or their age, but the data shows they're not. Data – now that's a topic that we'll be revisiting regularly over the coming chapters.

It doesn't work that way, and that's the most important point of all to pull out of it. These characteristics are not linked to education or upbringing.

The other important factor to consider here is the direction of travel, which can only work one way. You can transition from a Settler to a Prospector, or a Prospector to a Pioneer, but you can't go backwards. Once the shift has been made, you can never become a Settler again.

Why is it so important for managers to recognise and understand these cultural dynamics? Because these groups of people will have very different triggers, which means that every time you are putting a message out there, you are running the risk of alienating two thirds of them.

How do you avoid this? By couching your message in different forms of vocabulary, focal points, or tone. Otherwise, trust me, there's a very high probability that you'll find yourself pissing off two thirds of the population you're talking to at any one time.

We all need to wise up to this.

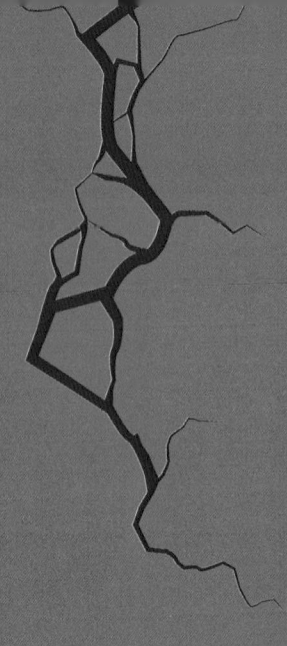

"Nothing is perfect. Life is messy. Relationships are complex. Outcomes are uncertain. People are irrational."
Hugh Mackay

CHAPTER *two*

The obvious is an antidote to curiosity

Dale Carnegie, the author of How To Win Friends and Influence People, once said: "When dealing with people, remember you are not dealing with creatures of logic, but creatures of emotion."

He preached a trilogy of key principles – building self-confidence, enhancing people skills, and developing communication skills.

Let's deal with that self-confidence point first. It's been reported that as many as 70% of us will experience 'imposter syndrome' at some point in our working lives.

This is the feeling that we're not good enough to be doing the job for which we are being paid; that we're pulling the wool over an employer's eyes, or flying by the proverbial seat of our pants.

The dictionary definition of imposter syndrome is 'the persistent inability to believe that one's success is deserved or has been legitimately achieved as a result of one's own efforts or skills'.

I think that one of the biggest culprits here is our inability to recognise or reflect on our successes; to keep the individual ingredients which make up our lives in perspective.

When something goes well for us – in either our personal or professional lives – we just take it in our stride, don't we? It's a very British thing not to want to come across as too boastful.

That's the paradox of contradictions raising its head again. It's exactly how I feel writing this; I can almost hear my (very pragmatic) father in the background saying to me: "If that's the way you think about it son, then why on earth are you writing it?"

It's that feeling of being overwhelmed by existential angst, which I suspect many of us will have experienced at some time or other.

Inwardly, though, should we instead be dwelling a little longer to dissect the winning formula? I certainly think so.

At the very least, reflect on and acknowledge all your hard work and carefully plotted strategy.

Yet lots of us – myself included – don't do this. Instead, we simply roll up our sleeves and say 'OK, that's finished, now what's next?' and it's a definite weakness.

Think of the precious intelligence that we have worked so diligently to accumulate, which is being cast on the scrapheap. Think of the useful ideas we've gained from our experiences which we should be committing into our memory banks.

We all have times in our lives when we are faced with a daunting, and frankly unattainable Everest rearing up in front of us. And it's at times like these that the memory banks can help us to remember how we reached the top of similarly daunting summits in the past.

My starting point when I was appointed chief executive of Shropshire Council can certainly be related to this. The county was facing its worst flooding for 25 years which caused heartbreaking destruction to homes and business premises.

And then, before we'd had any time at all to regroup, we were plunged straight into the worst global pandemic in living memory, trying to keep the economy ticking over against a backdrop of lockdowns, face masks and social distancing.

You do wonder at times like these how you are ever going to be able to find your way over such ferocious obstacles, but by separating each task, the tallest peaks don't appear quite so daunting.

> **For all the qualifications you may hold, there's sometimes no substitution for an honours degree from the University of Life.**

Experience tells you that the outcomes of every action you'll take, and any decision you'll make, are not binary. It's not as simple as saying you either did something, or you didn't. Got it right, or got it wrong. Oh for a world that was this straightforward...!

However you want to describe it, you can always put your successes or failures into perspective, or grade them on a scale of one to ten. And remember, no-one in the world gets everything right all the time, however much they might want to persuade you otherwise.

If you think you can be the exception, you are kidding yourself, and piling on extra unnecessary pressure. The result? You'll be doomed to consistently under-shoot your expectations and live in a constant state of frustration.

We all make illogical decisions at times. There's a fascinating book by behavioural economist Dan Ariely called 'Predictably Irrational' which explores the hidden forces which shape our day-to-day decisions.

You can create the best process in the world with the most logical steps, only to find it turns to shit the minute you insert people into it. Why? Because we're irrational, emotional, impulsive and unpredictable. Our beliefs and expectations infuse our opinions and decisions.

The kicker here, though, is that this phenomenon is wholly predictable, and by unpicking some of these patterns, and factoring this behaviour into your plans, you'll find yourself making better decisions in business.

You can see this in every walk of life. As Dan suggests in his book, irrationality often supplants rational thought and the reason for this is embedded in the very structure of our minds.

Which brings me onto another really important point. When it comes to trying to break a project down into manageable elements and put your aims and objectives into some sort of order, who exactly should you listen to for advice?

Should it be the person who was first to summit their particular Everest? The person who did it in the most time-efficient way? Or the person who has shouted loudest and proudest about it ever since? Quite possibly the answer is 'none of the above'.

If there's something wrong with my central heating at home, I just want an expert plumber. When my car breaks down, I want a mechanic who knows and understands every piston and valve, and is familiar with my marque of motor.

If I want to understand how to climb mountains, I will no doubt relish the chance to speak to one of those intrepid adventurers who has charted a path to the top.

But what I don't necessarily want, to repeat that phrase from earlier, is a generalist living in a specialist world.

Imagine how irritating and intolerable life would be if we filled our offices, friendship groups and social circles with people who were obsessed with one-upmanship and had an insatiable, egotistical appetite for adventure . . . it would be like being trapped 24 hours a day inside an episode of The Apprentice without the ability to jab out the finger and say 'You're fired'!

I'm not for a moment saying that all of life's adventurers are simply doing it for glory and gratification – far from it in most instances, and there are many I truly admire.

What I'm really trying to emphasise here is that we should always have the nous to pick and choose our role models, and realise there will be different horses for different courses.

The 64,000 dollar question, of course, is how do we identify these people who have something valuable to say to us, and how do we know when the time is right to open our ears to them?

The world is full of shiny objects, and we certainly should not be overly influenced by the first one that we see. Be clear in your mind about precisely what it is you want from a mentor, before you start the mental selection process.

Everybody in this world has experience, and something to say, and I'm a firm believer that you can learn something from everyone. Listening is one of life's most important skills; there's a reason people have two ears and only one mouth!

But we have a habit these days of taking everything we are told on face value, without questioning its validity or provenance.

Remember, you don't have to take on board every theory that people present to you; in most cases it may just be a phrase, or an odd word, that resonates.

That's why I make no apology for making regular reference throughout this book to powerful paragraphs or one-liners from people of all walks of life. Think of them as triggers, or hooks, to send us on a particular train of thought.

> **People like management guru Peter Drucker, who proffers: "Management is doing things right . . . leadership is doing the right things."**

Now I'll wager that this is not the first 'management' publication you have ever thumbed through.

But I'm prepared to bet it's the first which will have been written by someone whose eclectic career has spanned roles as a DJ and doorman to YTS garage mechanic, labourer, funeral driver, holiday park bluecoat, car paint salesman, hospitality manager, restaurant owner and care assistant. Yes, that really is all on my CV.

Why do I bring this up? Maybe because it demonstrates my background as someone with a work ethic who was prepared to have a crack at anything, not afraid to follow my instincts, and to go with what felt right at the time?

An example that there is rarely a straight line in anyone's career path.

It's true to say that I never knew what I wanted to be when I grew up. In fact, I probably don't really know even now. That's OK though, isn't it?

We no longer live in a world where people throw all their eggs into one career basket – quite possibly following one of their parents' footsteps – and then stick with it until they depart with a gold watch for long service, a plaque on the boardroom wall, and a final salary pension.

We don't even want a job with regular working hours these days, do we? For fear of feeling stuck in some sort of Groundhog Day rut. Why is that? Is it because our minds are wired up differently these days, or because our priorities in life have simply changed by having our eyes opened to what sort of work-life balance is possible? Almost certainly the latter, I'd venture.

People often get boxed into careers or vocations – or indeed do it to themselves. And that's frustrating, because when you lift the lid of that box and unpick the construct, people that you maybe perceived as single-faceted so often end up transforming into butterflies and become really talented individuals. All they needed was to be given the opportunity, or the belief, that they could be or do anything different.

Working with those kinds of people, and helping them to develop their untapped skills to realise their maximum potential, is what it's all about. It's incredibly rewarding, engenders loyalty and a real team spirit, and gets repaid hundreds of times over.

Reciprocity, they call it: exchanging things with other people to receive a mutual benefit. Ensuring that you give people help when they need it, and unlocking doors to allow them to blossom, means they will get things done that they would never have achieved on their own, and all for the greater good.

Ancient Greek philosopher Aristotle famously said that the highest or best form of friendship involves a relationship between equals – one in which a genuinely reciprocal relationship is possible – describing reciprocity as 'true justice in exchange'.

It allows people to get things done that they would not be able to do on their own. So why wouldn't you?

If you are lucky enough to help people to blossom in this way, I have so many examples of how they come back to you and say: "Do you remember when you said or did this for me, which helped to set me on my way?"

Sometimes I don't remember (back to that issue of needing to be 'in the moment' so you can reflect on and analyse what we do or say in more detail) but it's something which has resonated with them so powerfully.

Actually, I think we're much better at seeking feedback on our actions and achievements these days. Maybe that's partially because we're going to probably get it anyway whether we like it or not, from the army of keyboard warriors just itching for the opportunity to pounce from their anonymous online ivory towers!

It's also commonplace these days, when you have used a company or bought a product, to receive a survey asking you to mark them out of 10.

Well-meaning as that is, it's so often flawed. Not the sentiment or motivation, but the way that the survey is constructed.

For example, you might ask me how I rated your service, and I'd have to give it a 10 out of 10. However, the service I received may have been the service I wanted or requested, rendering the question irrelevant!

People can often be blinded to this, or guilty of cutting and pasting a standard questionnaire which has little thought about how the answers need to be used for the benefit of your own business.

What's the point of getting the answers that you want, to questions you shouldn't be asking?

If that's you, then good luck putting that into some semblance of strategic business plan to move you forward.

> **I can't overstate the importance of being curious. The hardest curiosity, sometimes, is when you are not particularly enamoured with someone, or find them difficult to communicate with because their values or personalities may be diametrically opposed to your own.**

To remain curious, and to engage with people like this, is so difficult. And yet the benefits of putting in the hard yards to try to see things from their side of the fence can be immense.

The misappropriated belief that you are always right, is naïve, and will come back to bite you.

I really like the Tim Minchin quote which succinctly sums up much of this thinking in his typically frank and colourful turn of phrase:

"Opinions are like arseholes, in that everyone has one. There is great wisdom in this, but I would add that opinions differ significantly from arseholes, in that yours should be constantly and thoroughly examined."

"Accept that some days you are the pigeon, and some days the statue."
Dilbert

CHAPTER *three*

Pareto, Dilbert, and perceptions of wisdom

I'd like to introduce you to two colourful, outspoken, and dramatically different people: one goes by the name of Pareto, and the other's called Dilbert.

Let's start with Pareto. His mathematically-rooted principle states that for many of the key outcomes in this world, roughly 80% of consequences come from just 20% of causes. In other words, a relatively small percentage of influencers will have a massively over-exaggerated effect on our lives.

Why do we need to know this in business? Because it allows us to manage our time more efficiently, and identify which initiatives to prioritise for maximum impact. Don't sweat the small stuff, as the jargon-lovers would say.

The theory was actually created by a Romanian-born, American-domiciled management consultant Joseph Juran, but has its roots in the musings of an Italian polymath called Vilfredo Pareto.

He observed that around 80% of his country's land was owned by just 20% of the population and pondered how the roles of 'the vital few and the useful many' were shaping the world in which he lived.

Then there's good old Dilbert, who is certainly no theologian or mathematician, but became a cult hero through his appearance in comic strips which were first published in the late 1980s.

The Dilbert principle invites us to buy into the idea that if people stick around long enough, the most ineffective workers in any organisation will always end up being systematically moved to the place where they can do the least damage — positions of management.

Why? Because company owners don't want the least competent, least smart people to be trusted doing the actual legwork or, heaven forbid, representing the brand by interacting with customers at the coal face.

Dilbert is actually a hapless, fictitious engineer created by satirist Scott Adams, who invites us to believe that leadership is just nature's way of 'removing morons from the productive flow'.

You're smiling now, aren't you? Because you've seen this process in action…

The character has been lifted out of the comic strip world and spawned dozens of books, not to mention an animated TV series, merchandise, and even a video game. In some warped parallel universe, I reckon he'd be good mates with David Brent!

The Dilbert principle isn't an entirely original train of thought though; it has many parallels with something called the Peter principle which had previously argued that workers are promoted based on success until they attain their 'level of incompetence' and are no longer successful.

Why do we link Pareto and Dilbert here? To provoke a discussion about the different approaches taken by the two – which in many cases reach a broadly similar conclusion.

The Peter principle invites us to believe that people are initially promoted on merit with sound business logic, only to almost inevitably eventually over-shoot their capabilities and be stuck in jobs where they become over-paid and under-qualified corporate corks, blocking the career progression paths of talented colleagues.

I bet you've encountered at least one of these managerial mischief-makers in your time, and know exactly what I'm talking about. If they block the bottleneck for long enough, the company will start to haemorrhage its most talented people.

So joking and comic strips aside, there is a really serious and potentially damaging impact here. It's based around a concept called negative selection, which is most commonplace in organisations with rigid and clear hierarchies.

The theory goes something like this: An over-promoted person at the top needs to protect their position, and does so by surrounding themselves with lieutenants with just enough competence to perform their roles, but insufficient nous to embarrass or topple the manager from their perch.

Inevitably, this means that over the course of time, ambition among workers is stifled, morale hits rock-bottom, loyalty is tested to breaking point, and the organisation becomes far less effective as it is suspended in a position of stalemate.

> **How do you know if you're being managed by one of these blockers? Trust your instinct – it's usually right.**

Alternatively, try a game of 'bullshit bingo', which I find is often a good way of exposing the imposters, and breaking some of the inevitable pent-up frustration.

They'll be managers who talk in soundbites about 'leveraging buy-in', 'boiling the ocean', 'sweating the asset', 'deep-diving into strategy', 'picking the low-hanging fruit' or 'giving 110%'. And don't even get me started about saying 'it is what it is'.

(This is the part where I frantically go back and proof-read what I've written so far to make sure I'm in the clear...!!!)

People too often hide behind jargon like this as a substitute for hard, clear, and original thinking about their goals and ambitions.

I'm not advocating that bullshit bingo is the singular litmus test to a manager's abilities, but it can be a lot of fun.

The environment in which we live and work has changed so dramatically over the past few years, due to globally seismic events. We're still feeling the aftershocks right now, and life is changing at a pace none of us have seen in our lifetimes.

But this is when the brightest of people start to see opportunities. They start to reshape their roles to put themselves in pole position to capitalise.

I suffer from imposter syndrome to this day. I don't know anyone who, if they have taken a really honest look at themselves, doesn't from time to time. Right at the start of this process I hesitated and asked myself: "Is anybody going to be interested in anything I've got to say?"

Yet we're not supposed to have feelings like this, are we? Even less to own up to them. Traditional wisdom suggests it's a sign of weakness.

I don't agree with that. I never have. There's absolutely nothing wrong with questioning yourself, because it keeps you grounded. Keeps you learning.

Are managers, chief executives and company owners supposed to have the answers to everything? Of course not. And in my book, it takes a much stronger person to admit sometimes that they don't know something, and seek help from a more junior colleague.

Far from exposing a chink in your armour, it's showing people that their views matter, whatever their role in an organisation, and that you're open-minded to examples of all the best practice available to you, so you can do the best possible job with everyone's interests in mind.

It should never be about who comes up with an idea – only about how wise that idea is. Teamwork, I think they call it.

Like Dilbert, I'm no mathematician, but apparently seven is the magic number in life. Don't ask me why, but it's what we're always led to believe. The Magnificent Seven; The Secret Seven; the Seven Wonders of the World; Double-O Seven.

"To err is human.
To really screw up requires a plan."

Some boffins believe that there are specific properties of the number seven that make it more appealing to people.

Mathematician Alex Bellos says: "Seven is the only number among those we can count on our hands that cannot be divided or multiplied within the group. We're always sensitive to arithmetical patterns, and this influences our behaviour."

I suppose the fact I'm even talking about this sort of proves the point. But why I really raise it is to emphasise the fact that people will jump on a fad, a trend or a buzzword if they think it's going to increase the chances of grabbing our attention.

You'll find lots of examples of 'seven top tips to success...' in self-help books, because it's perceived that this magic number makes the list somehow more appealing, more memorable, and more compelling. How? Why? Really?

It's fascinating to explore the difference between those who have the nous to process what they are being told, and others with a slavish addiction to a populist fad, or myth.

Not to mention those who jettison a perfectly good idea and leave it gathering dust for decades until someone comes along, gives it a shiny new coat of paint, and presents it as brand new.

Here's a perfect example. I'm reminded of a story which, if strictly true, I find quite incredible. In the days before the First World War, Japan learned about production line engineering from the Americans for the motor car, and took all of this knowledge back to Japan.

Decades later, with the motor industry in full flow, America then went back to Japan to learn 'the Toyota way', which they brought back to introduce into the USA's car production industry.

Yet it was the Americans who had taught the Japanese all about this in the first place, only to presumably leave that knowledge dormant, and forget about it. Go figure, as they would say.

There's a really important element in the Toyota model which merits reference here, and it's the fact that any worker on that production line could press the 'red button' to bring production to a halt.

Think about it. A multi-million pound process could be stopped in its tracks by the most junior of employees if they felt it necessary. Toyota believes that as long as you're the right person in the right place on the production line, you'll be the most qualified to know if something needs to change.

One of the key foundations of the Toyota Production System is "jidoka", loosely translated as automation with a human touch. When a problem occurs, the equipment stops immediately, preventing defective products from being produced.

Toyota says: "Jidoka means that a machine must come to a safe stop whenever an abnormality occurs. Achieving jidoka, therefore, requires building and improving systems by hand until they are reliable and safe.

"First, human engineers meticulously build each new line component by hand to exacting standards, then, through incremental kaizen (continuous improvement), steadily simplify its operations.

"Eventually, the value added by the line's human operators disappears, meaning any operator can use the line to produce the same result. Only then is the jidoka mechanism incorporated into actual production lines.

"Through the repetition of this process, machinery becomes simpler and less expensive, while maintenance becomes less time consuming and less costly, enabling the creation of simple, slim, flexible lines that are adaptable to fluctuations in production volume."

It sounds such an obvious thing to do when you put it like this, doesn't it? Moving the decision-making process away from the core function of a business is dangerous. Effective decision making needs to be contextual, connected . . . and continuous.

It gets me thinking about origins, and just how important it is to explore and acknowledge them.

Identifying and understanding your cultural background, and where you came from, is a powerful tool for creating a strong sense of belonging, and clarity of thought.

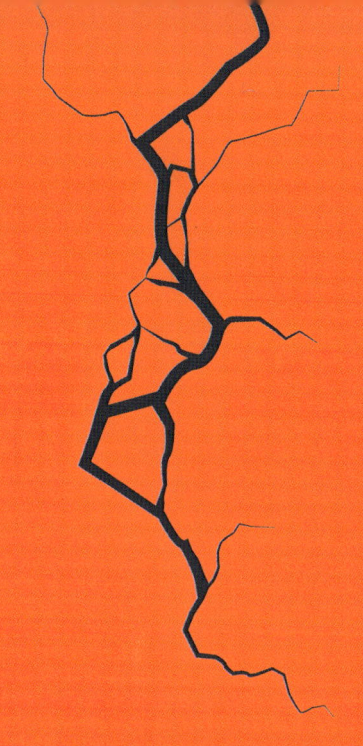

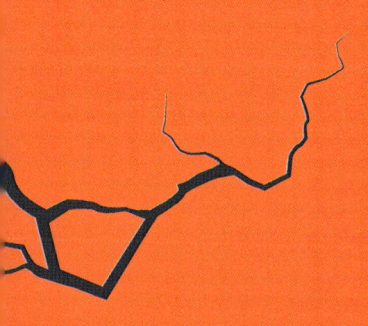

"Happiness is like an orgasm: if you think about it too much, it goes away. Keep busy and aim to make someone else happy, and you might find you get some as a side effect."

Tim Minchin

CHAPTER *four*

The sun will still rise if the cockerel doesn't crow

I'm a sucker for a good biography. Reading about other people's lives and adventures is something I always find motivational and thought-provoking.

A lot of them are so-called 'futurologists' – people looking to explore predictions and possibilities about the future, and how they can emerge from what's happening right now in the present day.

Challenging yourself to see the world from the different – sometimes disruptive – perspectives which many of these authors provide is a real eye-opener.

There's a fascinating book by Tom Cartwright, for example, called 'Narconomics' which explores how drug cartels become so powerful and prosperous.

He concludes that they've learnt their most important messages from big business – brand value and franchising from McDonald's, supply chain management from Walmart, and diversification from Coca-Cola. The list goes on.

They face exactly the same strategic concerns as the world's mega-companies like Apple. And this means that if you really want to understand how they think and act, you have to use the very same grounding in economics that you'd apply to your own corporate sphere.

'Superfreakonomics' author, economist Stephen Dubner, ponders why most of these drug dealers still live with their mums. The answer, he says, is that the majority of them can't afford a mortgage because they're actually earning less than the minimum wage.

Just like the standard capitalist model, only the fattest of cats make the megabucks in the criminal underworld, and you have to be pretty near the top of the pyramid to be bringing home a decent wage.

I'm assuming that life in a Mexican drug cartel is a world away from your daily travails, but the story does serve to remind us of some of the immoveable truths and principles which apply whatever you are doing, wherever in the world you happen to be.

The most successful organisations will always find the quickest way from point A to point B, because it will be the most efficient.

It's what drug cartels are brilliant at doing, and yet I don't imagine too many of them will have read a lot of management books!

You need to consider what you can learn from all sorts of places.

Like him or loathe him, Donald Trump is another case in point. He realised when he moved into the White House that he didn't need all the spin doctors and strategists to tell him how to communicate with his supporters; he could just take to social media and use the sort of vocabulary and value sets that he knew would resonate with certain tranches of the population. It was the quickest route for him to get from A to B. He knew what he was doing, and realised he didn't need the traditional Washington machine to do it.

I think he's probably one person though that we can have no hesitation in genuinely branding a 'disruptor'.

While we're using analogies from the other side of the Atlantic, the American Civil Rights movement is an interesting case study too. Maybe not an obvious place to go looking for modern-day wisdom on management techniques . . . though that's the point of what I'm saying in this entire book really, isn't it?

The fact is it holds a wealth of insight around strategy, tactics, negotiation and political manoeuvring and contains a huge amount of information you can use on a day-to-day basis.

This was the first time that conversations in the White House were transcribed, so you have the earliest possible evidence of the tactics and strategies being used by the president and his team. It's so informative to analyse what has changed since then, and what's stayed the same.

I'm a firm believer that we need to strive to ensure the systems in which we operate are configured appropriately; we need to learn from everyone, past or present. If you are bright enough to unpick the system in which you work, or the system itself provides you with the opportunity, then you are much more likely to find yourself thinking that way.

I'm not convinced that anyone is so hard-wired that they are incapable of believing they can't develop as a person, or can't re-imagine a vision for progress.

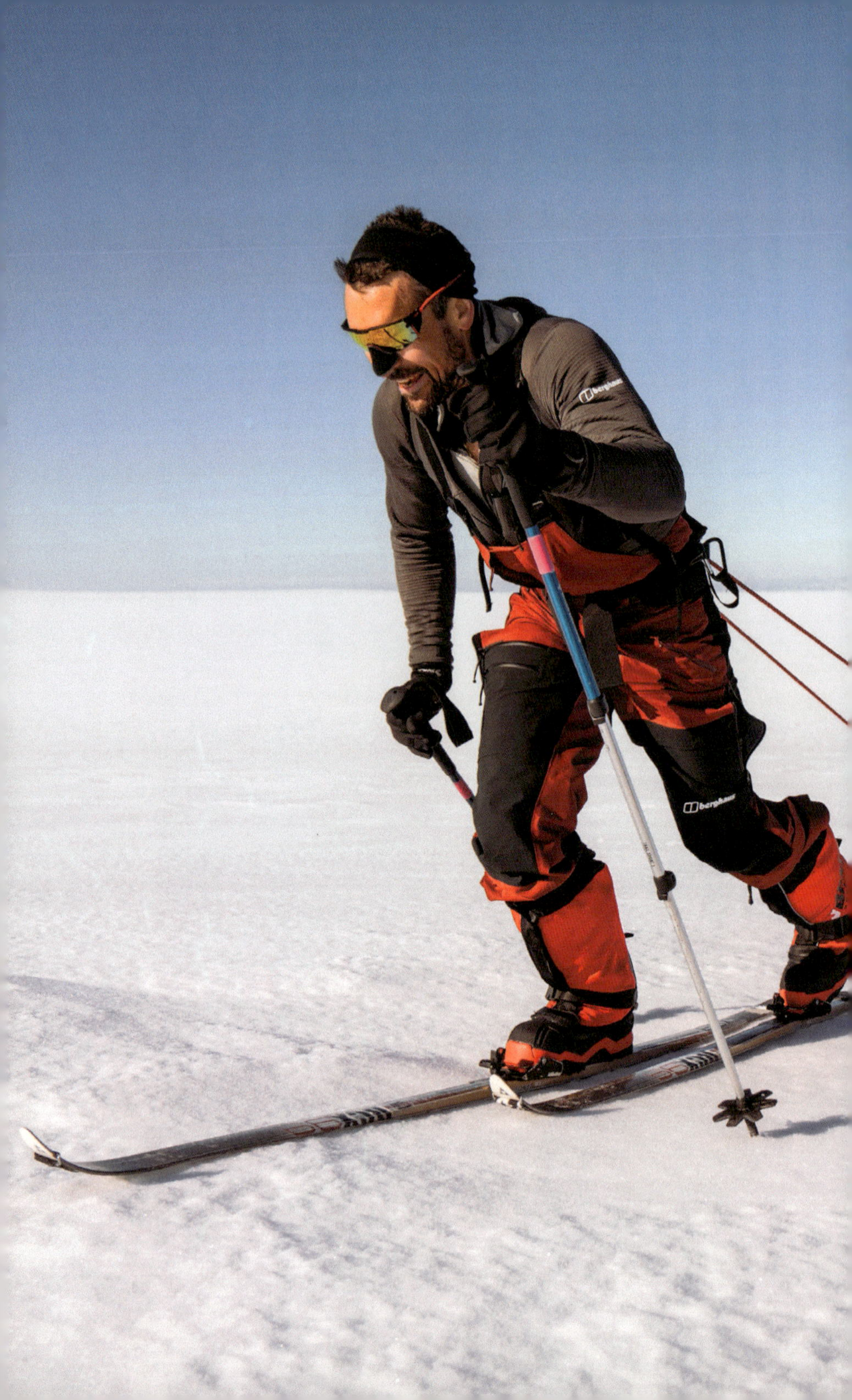

"Having started my career in local government, I often found myself frustrated by the lack of strong and effective leadership. When I first met Andy, I immediately recognised his empathetic, pragmatic, and strategic approach. Unlike many senior leaders, Andy leveraged the strengths of those around him and demonstrated the humility to acknowledge that successful leadership requires collective buy-in and ownership of the organisation's vision. In short, Andy's greatest skills as a leader are his empathy, humility, and ability to foster a shared vision that others embrace and take accountability for."

Darren Edwards

It's more likely that prevailing conditions are simply preventing them from opening their minds to it, and will be having a massive impact on their behaviours – probably much more than they appreciate.

I still find myself having to push into places where I don't really want to be; stepping into system conditions that are not comfortable, where I know I'll maybe hear some tough home truths. It's counter-intuitive, and at the time will be the last thing you want to do, but that's where development happens, and where learning takes place.

The message is: be careful which models you choose to follow, and for what purpose. Known unknowns seem to be the issues occupying a great deal of my time. Having said that, the more you put yourself out there, the more information you are going to be gathering to tackle whatever lies ahead.

There's an incredibly inspirational young man I'm fortunate to have got to know called Darren Edwards. I knew him early in his career when he had just left university and worked for me as a graduate recruit. He's a former mountaineer and Army reservist who sustained a life-changing injury in the summer of 2016 during a climbing accident.

Paralysed from the chest down, he was stripped of almost every aspect of the active, adrenaline-fuelled life he had been living.

It could have shattered his spirit, but instead he used it as a catalyst for growth. With grit, determination and an astonishing positivity, he has redefined the limits of what was thought possible for someone with a spinal cord injury. From becoming the first person with a disability to run seven marathons in seven days across seven continents in a wheelchair, to kayaking the length of Great Britain whilst leading a team of injured veterans; and following this with a ground-breaking expedition to sit-ski across Antarctica to the South Pole, he is living proof of the power of the human spirit in overcoming adversity, adapting to change, and finding a way from A to B.

There are seriously lessons we can learn from Darren's story, about what a robust mindset can achieve. As he says himself: "Beyond our own perceived limits lies our true potential."

> **There's an old French proverb which says: "The sun will still rise if the cockerel doesn't crow." The two occurrences are mutually exclusive. One does not rely upon the other. That's what they call a false positive.**

It's an analogy which I firmly believe can be used to help you with problem solving in your organisation.

Think about the system as a whole in your business, the context in which a particular problem sits – and challenge every single part of it.

In other words, if you are trying to make the metaphorical sun rise in your office every morning, appreciate that you don't need to fix the cockerel, because the role it is fulfilling is quite possibly not what you thought. You've just assumed that it is.

It may turn out that you don't need that cockerel at all, or can re-assign it to other more impactful duties. In an instant, you have just removed half of your resources and got the same outcome.

It turns my thoughts to the TRIZ methodology, the theory of inventive problem-solving, which is based upon logic, data and research, rather than on intuition.

It's the Russian acronym for the 'Theory of Inventive Problem Solving'. Inventor and science fiction writer Genrich Altshuller first wrote about it in 1946.

Whether it's right or wrong, there's no disputing the fact that it's really thought-provoking.

Essentially, he came to the conclusion that there is actually nothing new in the world, ever. It's just a question of putting the same basic ingredients together, maybe in a different order of priorities, and then resolving what he described as 'technical contradictions'.

I think there's definitely something in this; we are living our lives on a two-way axis and our task is to measure and connect the variables.

Often, this can only be done by employing a different way of thinking. But it's well worth taking the time and effort, because get it right, and it can speed up the problem-solving process.

It makes you appreciate that component parts of a problem are also essential parts of solving the problem.

It's a case of correlation and causation – fixing the cockerel won't make the sun rise any faster.

Take a can of Coca-Cola. It only works as a can if there is product inside it. It's only the pressurised liquid inside the can which makes it a great container. Without that pressurised liquid inside, the can becomes flimsy and useless.

It's about seeing the broader picture, and looking at it often from a different direction.

During my time in adult social care, I flipped the perception of the service from one which was seen as a black hole of money and resource that just eats up and consumes everything you throw at it.

Instead, I invited people to think about it in a different way, as one of the biggest drivers of the local economy because of the number of people it employs, and its GVA. When you think of it that way, it starts to take on a very different image.

I presented a detailed paper some years back to the Association of Directors of

Adult Social Services (ADASS) around the issue, when I chaired the West Midlands branch.

I wanted to shape the debate around the social care and health market, so we could predict and prevent demand and better utilise resources.

The problem we were trying to solve was quite simple: market fragility.

Because of an ageing population, we were seeing demand for social care services outstripping what the market could supply.

Focusing on the management of supply and demand, we began to look at how our input – the decisions we make – had a wider economic impact, positively affecting more than the council's core responsibility to meet the health and social care needs of our communities.

The result – a data visualisation tool the Bridge – empowered us to shape the market through smarter commissioning, and closer partnership with the likes of NHS Digital, the Local Government Association, ADASS, and various other partners.

By taking large datasets from health and social care and applying predictive analytics, artificial intelligence and deep learning, we were able to better understand the current demand in social care, allowing organisations to better predict and prevent future demand.

I firmly believed that this approach would help inform the way the council and its partners commissioned services in the future, leading to a more efficient use of resources and better outcomes for local communities.

Our journey started with ideas on how we could possibly turn adult social care into a driver of the local economy, rather than a drain.

Economist Sherman Wong was commissioned to look at the wider economic impact of health and social care. In his report he showed how the health and social care industry is one of the most economically valuable sectors in the region.

The findings of this report gave way to long discussion about how we could effectively calculate the economic value of commissioning decisions to help us make them more effectively. The process was lengthy and resource intensive, requiring more data on market supply and demand. The big challenge for us was to look at how we could better use and model our data and present it in a way which would engage with the user and allow them to interact with it.

> **But the idea of 'flippin' adult social care in this way certainly caught the imagination.**

It was, and remains, a good calling card to spark thought-provoking debate. I've since used the same tactic with 'Finding Dave', which we'll explore later.

There you go . . . that is me being openly tactical with you again!

Quotes, snippets and ready-to-use soundbites are so important. Not just to use, but to engage people in a train of thought.

So often in business, I find that a problem lies in very close proximity to a solution. It's just finding it. Looking at it through a different lens can bring clarity.

It brings me back to that customer service questionnaire issue again – it's no good wasting time searching, unless you are asking the right questions.

There's a model called the 'Five Whys' which is used by many large organisations, including the health service, and it's a good path to follow.

It's a tool to help uncover the root cause of a problem that has occurred during a project or programme by repeatedly asking the question 'why' has something been done. Why is one of the most important questions you can ever ask.

Sometimes, though, you may not know what the question is that you should be asking – and it's important not to be afraid of a scenario like this.

Observe a system, study the data, look at all the component parts and start questioning what each piece of your jigsaw should be telling you. Is it delivering?

If you're measuring the wrong things and hoping that this will improve your predicament, it's never going to happen. What's the old adage? Weighing a pig doesn't make it get fatter…

These days we have much more information at our fingertips. Think about what happens when you layer that information; it can start to tell you some incredible things that you have never seen before – you've just got to be open enough to go looking for it in the first place.

With the rapid development in Artificial Intelligence, you can lay an almost infinite number of data sets on top of one another, which are crying out to be asked the right questions.

Sometimes it's a case of showing people a scenario in a different way. An example I've used is to engage with people in a 360 degree environment, projecting information in the round to a group of say a couple of dozen people at a time.

It engages people in a different way to anything I've ever seen before. A floor-to-ceiling presentation in a different setting like that does so much more than a spreadsheet ever can.

It's about taking time to understand what might stimulate people . . . and appreciating the differences between strategy, and tactics, with good communication also an absolute must.

There will be times when your team members can work things out that you simply can't, but you have got to get them in the right head space to make the magic happen, then be open minded enough to listen.

People find uncertainty incredibly uncomfortable, but I think to a certain degree you have got to learn to change your mindset and be comfortable with it. Because once you are, you relax into it, let your guard down, open your mind, and appreciate that it's perfectly OK not to know the answer, or to be unsure about which direction we need to head next.

It reminds me of that oft-misquoted speech by former US defence secretary Donald Rumsfeld, who said: "There are known knowns; there are things we know we know. We also know there are known unknowns; that is to say we know there are some things we do not know. But there are also unknown unknowns – the ones we don't know we don't know."

It sounds like strategic spaghetti, but it's actually a really useful model to help understand risk and manage some complex environments.

Today's world is complex, chaotic, and unpredictable – more so than ever. Let's liberate our minds and accept that these are the parameters in which we have to live every day.

The uncertainty becomes the certainty.

"*When you're on top of your game, change your game.*"

James Kerr, Legacy

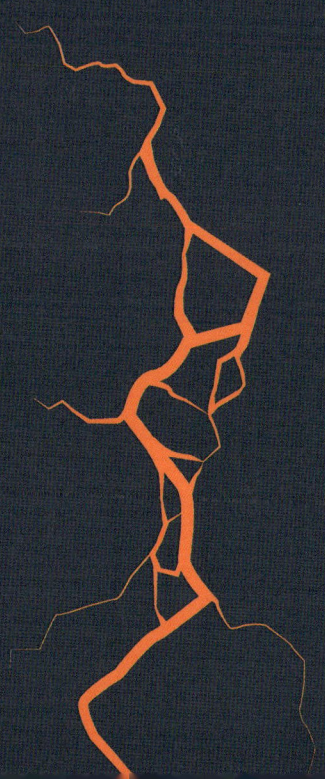

CHAPTER *five*

Custodians of culture... and rule number seven

You don't have to be a fanatical sports fan to succeed in life, but I do believe it can give you a significant helping hand along the way.

Whether playing or spectating, it offers an outlet for your physical and mental pressure... a cause to bond over, and passionately follow with your friends and colleagues... and a fantastic classroom for honing your management and coaching skills.

The business of sport is almost unrecognisable from the environment it operated in before the end of the 20th century.

Back then, controlling bodies were typically run in an amateurish way, with a closed-shop, top-down governance structure which made it crystal clear that adhering to tradition would always trump the need for transformation.

Not any more. There have always been common strands linking top sporting teams and the most successful businesses, but I believe the 21st century sporting arena can teach us more than ever about our colleagues, our companies, and ourselves.

Growing up, my number one sport was always rugby, and it remains one of my passions to this very day. There was no better sport for a young man, brimming with testosterone, to run round and get it out of his system. But there's so much more to the game than that; it's specifically designed so that players of all shapes and sizes can compete on the same level playing field against each other, with a sense of fairness. Just like you'll find in pretty much any business.

Rugby taught me the basics of discipline, the essence of teamwork, and the importance of putting faith in other people. First you do your bit correctly, then you rely on others to do the same. When that happens, more often than not you end up winning, celebrating, bonding, and feeling really good about life.

And this is where the philosophy feeds back into any field of business. Get the basics right, create a culture of everyone pulling together for a shared goal, and you'll be surprised how powerful and motivational it can prove to be.

Sometimes, of course, it's easier to create this culture on a sports field than in a boardroom, because you're all entirely focused on the opposition in front of you, and have the same goals to achieve in the same timeframe as everyone else on your side. Business is more nuanced than this. But the principles are still sound.

If you want to excel and improve, you've got to constantly analyse and dissect your performance, individually and collectively, and chase the sort of 'marginal gains' that you hear the likes of the world's top cycling, sailing or motor racing teams speak of. At the top level of sport – and indeed business – it's the fine tuning which makes the champions really shine.

One of the mantras of the all-conquering New Zealand All Blacks was: "When you are on top of your game, change your game."

I like that. It's a really unusual message in management terms. Why would you change when you are successful?

Companies like Marks & Spencer could probably have done with advice like that in the 1990s when, after being on top of their game and kings of their marketplace for decades, they failed to appreciate that while they were staying the same, competitors were coming up fast on the rails with new products and ideas, and ended up leaving them behind.

I looked on with admiration at the way Sir Clive Woodward turned around the entire fortunes of English rugby – a juggernaut of a system, steeped in tradition and stuck in its ways, which needed to be persuaded that it was time for reinvention.

There were some brutally frank, divisive and difficult conversations to be had in those early months, but the silverware in the cabinet – the 2003 Rugby World Cup – was the ultimate proof that it was all worthwhile.

Could that success possibly have been achieved without the major overhaul which Sir Clive's vision and determination spearheaded? We'll never know for sure of course, but I don't believe so.

Sir Clive had to tell the Rugby Football Union some uncomfortable home truths in his quest to change the attitudes of the top brass from an amateurish approach to one of progressive professionalism.

He not only worked with the team to get them on side, but had to shake up a very traditional, controlling and at times rather secretive organisation at the same time. In other words, he had to manage both up the chain to his shareholders, and down the line to his front-line workforce.

Sir Clive says: "Our success was not a continual series of victories. We had a number of devastating setbacks – how these are handled is the making of a great team. Winning does not happen in straight lines."

So true. We've touched on this already – not dwelling too long on the dark days,

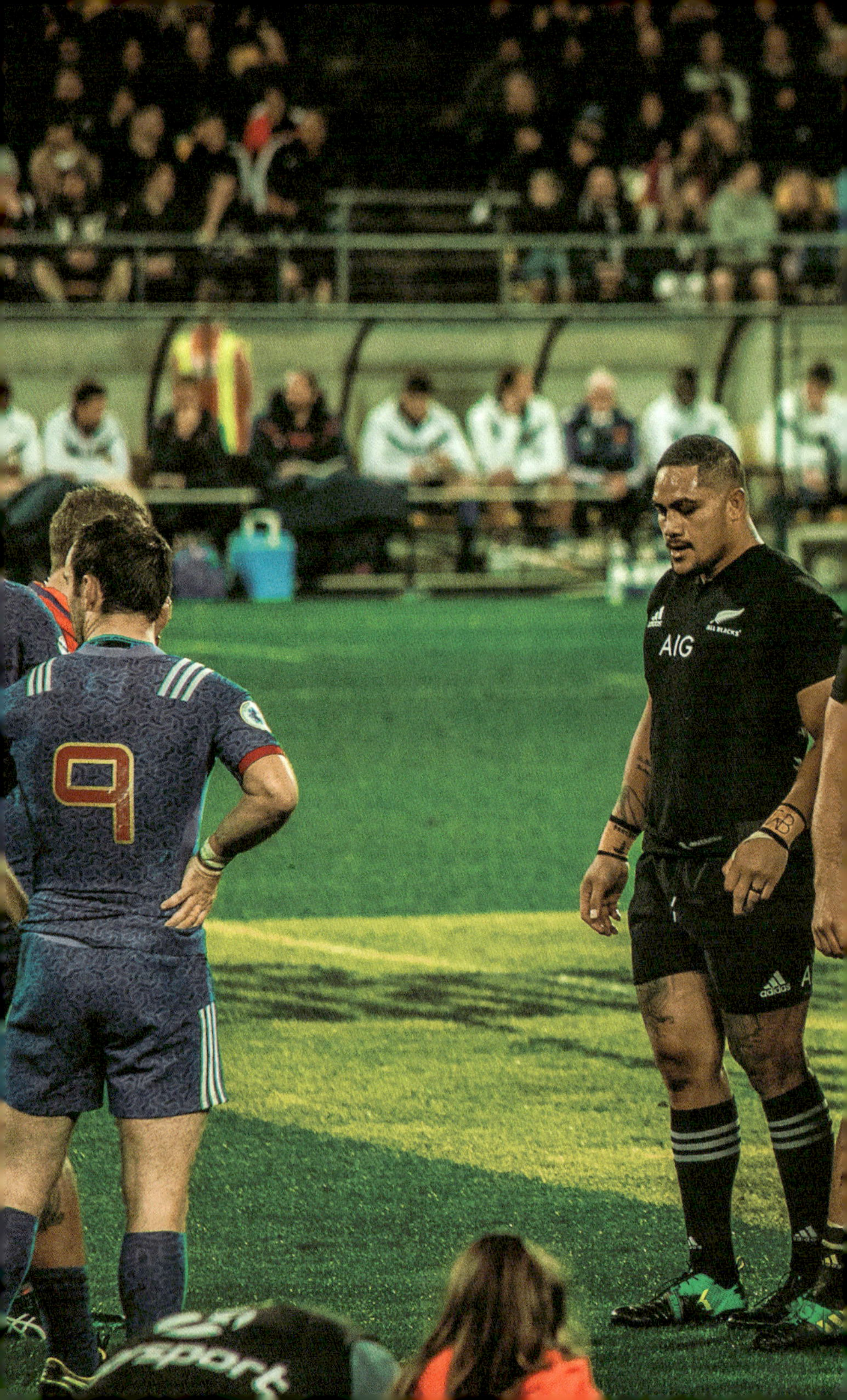
AIG
9
adidas

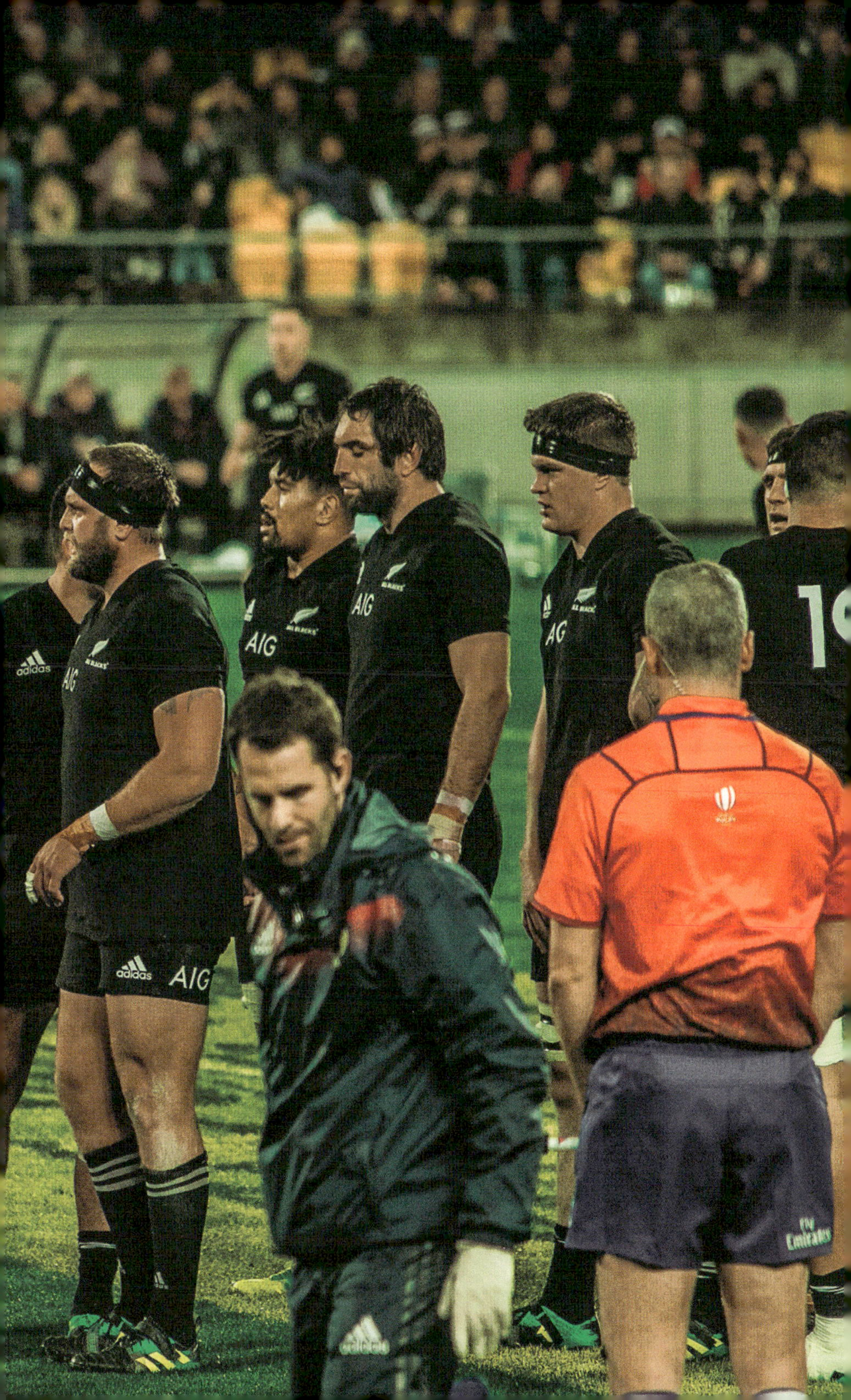
AIG
adidas
19

but picking up useful pointers and storing them in the memory banks. Any manager will tell you that they learn more from a defeat than they do from a victory.

Sir Clive believed that concentrating too long on simply measuring performance, in the hope that winning would then take care of itself, was a 'brilliant excuse for coming second', and felt it was imperative that captain and coach were always banging the same drum.

It's not rocket science, is it? But I believe there are so many powerful lessons to be learned here, particularly around how collaborative and dynamic leadership will always get the best out of an entire team.

What is it that wise old Aristotle said? A team can be greater than the sum of its collective parts.

And the ability to cut straight to the chase is an important tool here. Take, for example, New Zealand's all-conquering All Blacks whose mental skills coach revealed one of the squad's golden rules – no dickheads in the dressing room! Rule seven, they call it.

Simple, straightforward, and completely embraced by the players, it immediately filtered out inflated egos and made everything about the collective, rather than the individual. I bet you can think of several scenarios in your own working life when just such a rule would have come in quite handy!

It's also said that the All Blacks are the only international team in the world who still sweep their own dressing rooms and tidy up before they leave. It's rule one – 'sweep the sheds'. No coincidence, I'd venture to suggest.

You are never too big to do the small things.

The moment that you have people who feel certain tasks are beneath them, who put themselves ahead of the team, or believe they are entitled to certain privileges and feel the rules should be somehow different for them, you're allowing a wedge to be driven straight through the heart of your operation. It can have a catastrophic and wide-reaching impact.

Sometimes, it might not be the managers themselves who spot the warning signs first – which is why it's vital that you are able to foster a culture where your 'players' feel it's OK to put their heads above the parapet and call these people out before the decay has chance to spread.

If your staff can see something going wrong, but feel they are not able or welcome to voice their concerns to those in positions of power, your business is doomed to failure. Simple as that.

Nelson Mandela used the power of sport to heal, inspire and unite an entire nation. That day when he appeared wearing a Springbok jersey in that famous rugby World

Cup final was an iconic moment, and a reminder that sport really does have the power to change the world.

There's a powerful management concept which is worthy of mention here; the importance of 'catching people doing something right'.

And we're not just referring here to a glib and shallow 'thanks team' when you walk into the room. It needs to get down to the nitty-gritty, to prove to your colleagues that you really are paying attention to the work they are doing, and the difference they are making.

For example, thanking someone for a specific input into a project, or piece of data provided, and outlining to them what it had helped the business to achieve. If any boss of yours has ever done this to you, I'll bet it remains one of the most vivid memories you cherish from your time working with them.

Don't think this is just one-way traffic either. No boss in the world wouldn't welcome a similar sentiment from one of their colleagues, rubber-stamping their managerial and motivational skills.

So, against this powerful backdrop, the question is why would you not use sport and the essence of good teamwork as a blueprint to improve parts of your own business?

We all want to create a culture which promotes and strives for success. And all the boardroom strategies and managerial masterplans in the world can't achieve this alone.

Sport is also a brilliant example of overcoming the kind of cultural barriers which can often hold a business back. If we switch focus from rugby to football for a minute, just look at the way Dutch coach Sarina Wiegman took the England Lionesses by the scruff of the neck and transformed them into European champions and World Cup finalists.

"I really wanted to share who I really am, what my vision is, how I work with people, how I think of training and things like that," she said when asked what motivated her to take on the role.

She'd never had milk in her tea or tried fish and chips before she came here, but her determination to learn about our culture immediately endeared her to the players and made them think: if she's making these sort of sacrifices and putting in all this effort, the least we can do is to follow her. A winning culture, and that collective feeling of teamwork, can be almost unbreakable. So ask yourself, who's the custodian of culture in your organisation? Could it be you? Should it be you?

Does what you are doing right now make your boat go faster? If it does, then do more of it. If it doesn't, set yourself on a different path of discovery.

It brings me back to something I mentioned a little earlier, around the importance of taking a few moments to pause and reflect on success or failure.

You can distil down success and failure at different points of your working week, and then revisit and reform your plan of attack in exactly the same way as a manager may do with their sporting squad.

Do you need to sign new players for your own squad, with a different set of skills to cope with the fast-moving business world? Yes, you do. The squad you had last season may have been capable of winning the league, but your competitors aren't going to roll over and let you have the trophy.

Do you need to constantly nurture and encourage younger people from your 'academy' structure to keep the production line flowing so star performers can be promoted into more senior roles. Yes, of course you do. The mixture of youthful energy and more mature wisdom will help your business to cover all knowledge bases.

Analogies between sport and business are around every corner, which is why I believe it can be an incredibly effective motivational tool.

The challenge, though, is how to get this across without immediately turning off and alienating nearly half the population who weren't born with that sporting gene. The best managers will tailor the delivery of the exact same message in many different ways.

I have incredible admiration for those successful coaches who go about things in a left-field way. People talk about them for generations as if they are some sort of super-human beings, but they're not. Just ordinary people doing extraordinary things, by being prepared to chart their own path. Risking failure in the search for the biggest success.

I've crossed paths in the past with 'liquid thinker' Damian Hughes, who combines his practical and academic background within sport, organisational development and change psychology to help create a high performing culture. Have a listen to his 'High Performance' podcast when you get a chance, because it offers an intimate glimpse into the lives of high-achieving, successful individuals. It doesn't matter whether the guests have excelled in sport, music, business or entertainment, they all have non-negotiable behaviours they have employed to get them to the top, and keep them there.

Damian has done a lot of work in the world of boxing, and spent time at the famous Kronk Gym in Detroit to find out why it has managed to produce such a disproportionately high number of world champions; names like Lennox Lewis, Thomas 'The Hitman' Hearns, Evander Holyfield, and Naseem Hamed.

As you can imagine, there was plenty of working-class testosterone being thrown around in there, but one of the coaches shared one important message, which was this:

"Unless I can calm a potential new recruit down, there's absolutely no point trying to do any teaching. Until they feel comfortable, and they are committed and focused, I'm wasting my breath because nothing I say before that point will ever soak in."

> **Making colleagues feel at ease is, in my opinion, one of the most important managerial lessons of all.**

You don't realise in your everyday life how inadvertently under stress you can sometimes make people feel.

If the chief executive picks up a phone and says he would like to speak to a junior member of staff, their immediate reaction is: "Oh shit, what have I done?"

Maybe they actually just deserved a pat on the back and a pay rise…if you're a good manager, you won't just engage in dialogue with your staff when they need a stern talking-to.

The best managers are always the ones who have the self-awareness to appreciate how their actions, mannerisms and attitudes impact on the lives of others.

Harvard Business School professor and author Amy Edmondson coined the phrase 'psychological safety' – a shared belief held by members of a team that it is acceptable to take risks, to express ideas or worries, and to never be afraid to speak up if you have questions.

This can only work if colleagues can act without fear of negative consequences. If a project you're involved in isn't going to plan, it's natural to be worried about what the management will say.

Amy says: "There are many polite workplaces that don't have psychological safety, because there's no candour. People feel silenced by the enforced politeness. Unfortunately, at work, nice is often synonymous with not being candid."

Good bosses won't just ask what went wrong if a problem occurs, or how it could have been avoided. They'll also want to know what you've learned from the experience and how it can develop you as a person.

Not only will you feel relieved if your boss approaches the situation in this way, you'll also feel far more motivated, supported, engaged, and undoubtedly more comfortable to speak up in the event of a problem next time. Provided, of course, that you are indeed learning from each scenario.

For me, it boils down to this: who you've got on your team is actually far less important than how effectively the team is working together.

Successful teams are full of people who will have their colleagues' backs, because they realise that it's the best approach in the long run for everyone.

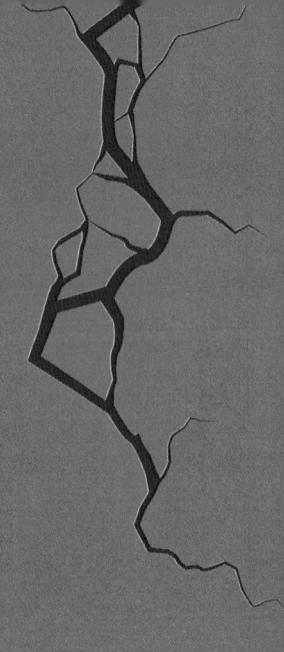

"Everything that irritates us about others can lead us to an understanding of ourselves."
Carl Jung

CHAPTER *six*

Certainty, uncertainty, discipline & hygiene

There's a rather agricultural but typically direct phrase uttered among folks up north which goes: "If you fell in a barrel of shit you'd still come out smelling of roses".

Or, in rather more delicate terms, you are a jammy so-and-so who always seems to get away with things, however great the odds might be stacked against you.

When I was scoring tries at rugby, people used to tell me it was lucky that I seemed to be constantly in the right place at the right time.

I'd reply to them: "It's funny, but the harder I train on a Tuesday and Thursday night, the luckier a player I seem to be!"

The best leaders are not just lucky; the results they achieve don't just happen by accident. Yes, they undoubtedly have a degree of latent talent, but they also put in a heck of a lot of effort that most people never get to see.

We train hard so that we can get the basics right. But more than that, we do it so that we can no longer get the basics wrong.

If you can't throw a rugby ball or catch a rugby ball, the best game plan in the world is never going to win matches.

One of my favourite phrases I use at work is 'discipline & hygiene' – getting the basics right in a business, and paying attention to the little things.

It's back to that question of why it's so important to smile at colleagues in the car park, or answering emails and communications courteously. Otherwise you are metaphorically 'dropping the ball'.

We've talked a lot already about the similarities between top-class sporting performers and successful business leaders on many levels, but there is one important difference.

World-leading sports people need a huge degree of confidence – some may say arrogance – to reach the pinnacle. They need to be selfish, ruthless, and tunnel-visioned . . . and this combination can be a dangerous cocktail in the boardroom.

In the business game, you need to balance this with tact, diplomacy, wisdom, and a gut feeling for knowing when the time's right to put your foot on the accelerator.

Learning how to bide your time, and only moving when the time is right, is one of the most important of all leadership skills.

It's about being aware of when you need to sit and listen to somebody else venting, and then understand when the moment has come to lay down your side of the argument.

If I'm engaged in a heated online discussion late in the day, I always try and check myself... I try to resist sending an email on impulse, probably because at times like this I tend to type with my fists. Pausing for a moment, or preferably sleeping on it is usually my course of action.

Nine out of 10 times, I'll actually be really calm when faced with a tricky situation, but there is an art to showing your anger at times, and for it to really have its intended impact I think you have to use it sparingly.

There is no use gaining a reputation as someone whose default position is to shout and swear at the top of their voice all the time, because you've then got nowhere to go if a situation really does call for a more forceful reaction.

> **It's the classic 'cry wolf' syndrome – if you go off like a firework every five minutes, then people won't believe you when there really is something which calls for an alarm.**

Colleagues of mine tell me they always know when I'm angry, which always surprises me, because I think I hide it quite well. Apparently not, and clearly I'd make a lousy poker player.

I'm not for a minute saying there is anything wrong with showing emotion though. I've been doing some self-reflection recently and come to the conclusion that maybe I don't do that enough – positively, or negatively.

Sometimes though, you can't escape the need for a dose of boardroom brutality.

However much you buy into the various theories we're exploring here around what makes the perfect manager, there will be moments when you have to say to yourself: "Fuck it, there's no way round this, I've got to just do it." (JFDI)

You know there will be consequences, but you have to deal with them. At the end of the day, that's what you're in the chair for.

There's a question which crops up in magazine Q&A articles quite often which I always think is an interesting one. It's the bit where they ask how you think your colleagues would describe you.

If it veers dramatically from the words you would use to describe yourself, then I'd say it's time to sit yourself down for some introspection, and deliver a few stern home truths.

> **Leadership is about authenticity. You are who you are, and should never try to be someone you're not. Put on an act, and it'll only be a matter of time before you get found out; then your credibility will be flushed down the drain.**

At the same time, though, you need to come across to colleagues as a human being and rounded individual, and not just the holder of a senior position. That can be quite challenging, particularly when you know that you will probably have to adopt a very challenging attitude at some point with colleagues in other leadership roles.

Ground rules have to be laid down. If you've ever been in a situation where you have worked with a colleague for a long time and your careers have since taken dramatically different pathways, you'll no doubt know what I'm saying, and why I raise this.

Some people excel at that side of people management, but others don't. Just because someone is a really good team player in a business, and is liked and respected by their peers, doesn't automatically make them a natural manager.

Some universities, particularly in the United States, believe they can start to nurture senior executives very early on in their learning journeys. Can it really be taught to anyone in such a regimented way? I'm not entirely convinced.

Take the famous 'staircase' diagram which is often used to chart progress. At the start of your career, you're always at the bottom looking up, and all you'll be able to see is the next step.

It's only when you get the top, to a point when your next move isn't planned out for you, that you're able to see the entire staircase for the first time by looking back down.

Hindsight, they say, is a wonderful thing – but I'd only buy into this sentiment to a degree.

It's a bit self-congratulatory to look down, pat yourself on the back and say 'haven't I done well?', but it can certainly help you to pinpoint times on your journey when there were pivotal moments where you maybe made the right decision, or a particularly bold decision, which shaped the person you have become.

Philosophically, of course, you never actually know whether you are making the right or wrong decision, because it was the only one you made at the time!

> **In reality, our journey through life is very non-binary. Being relaxed with uncertainty is so important.**

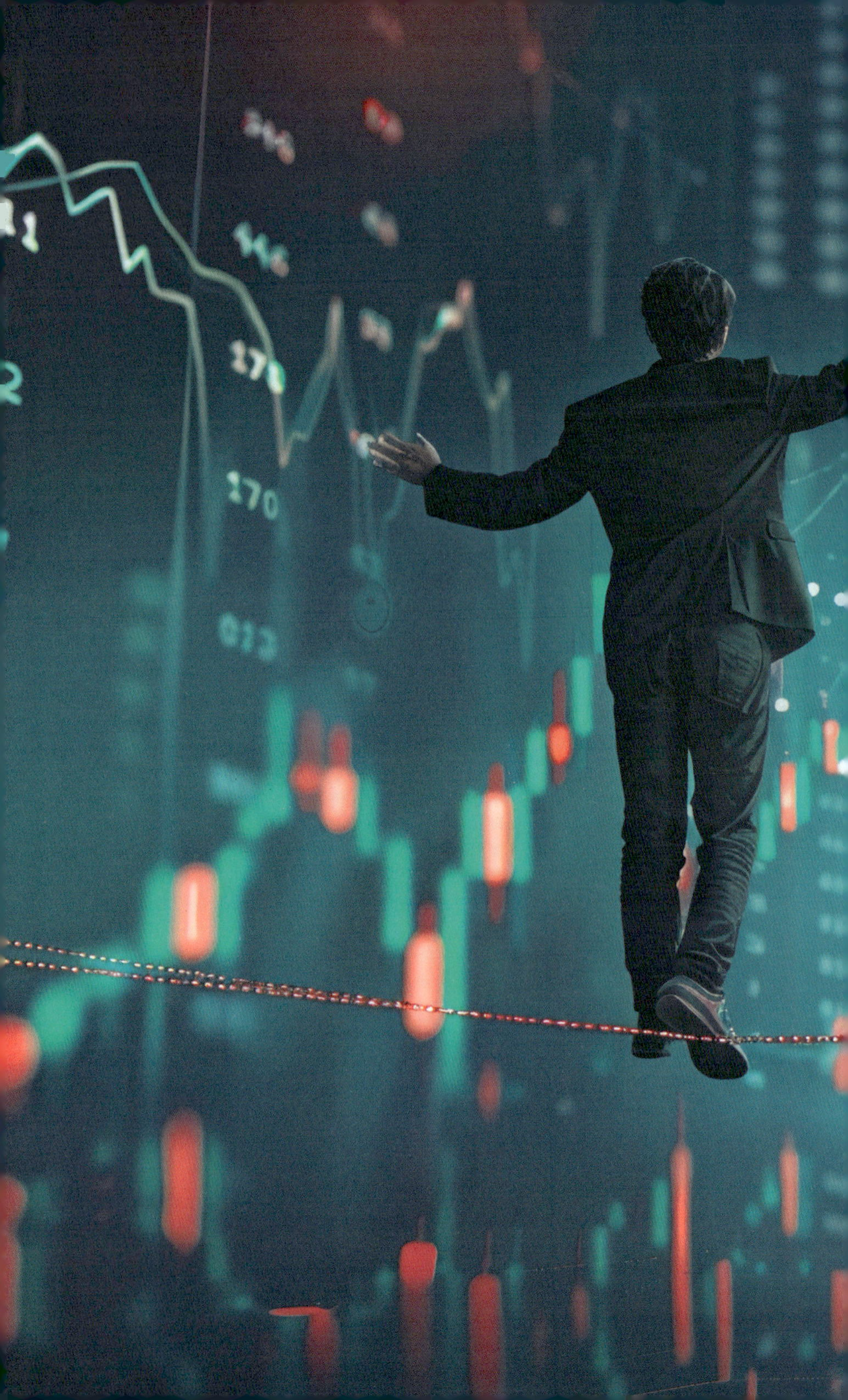

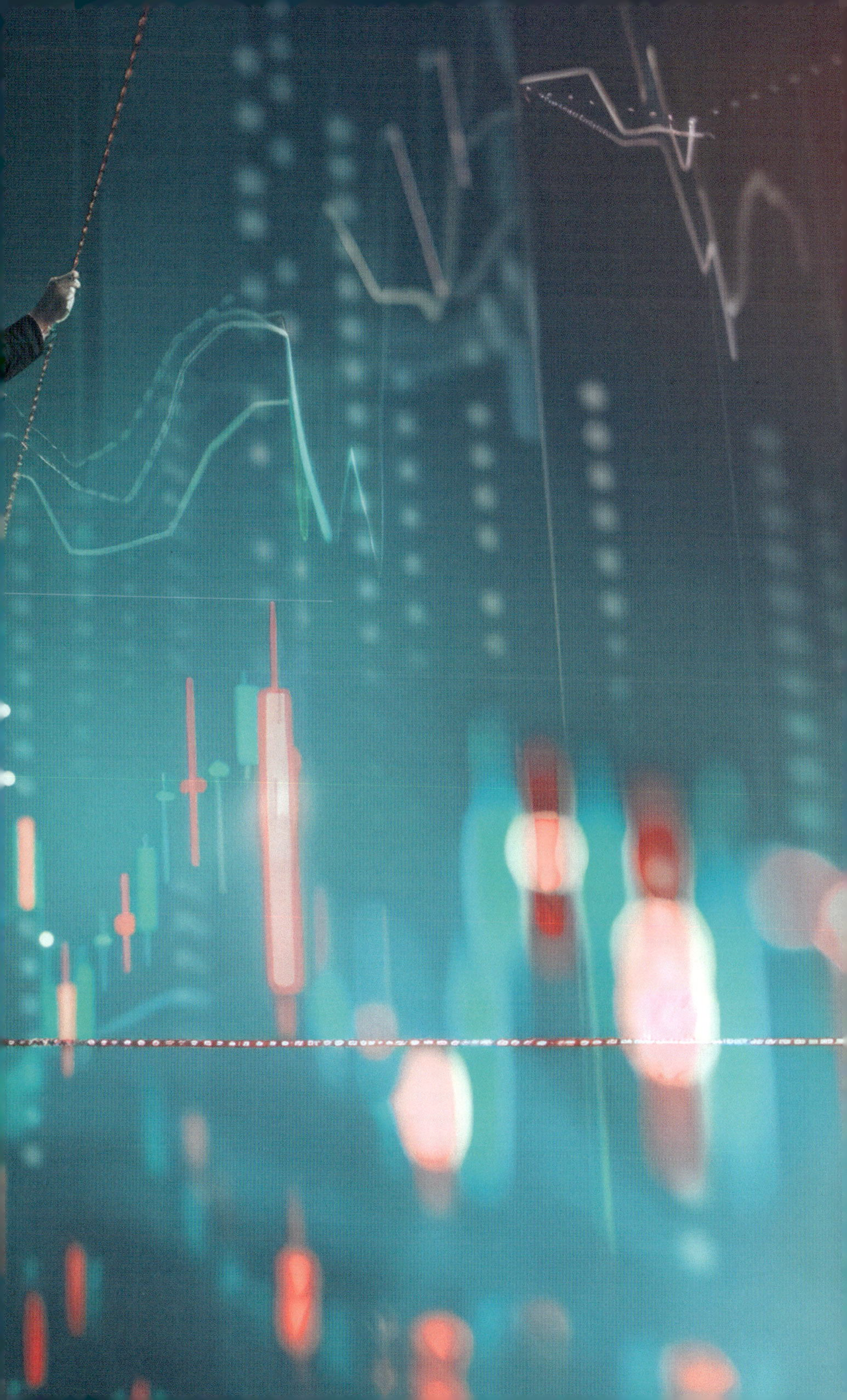

It keeps you grounded to recall the times when you either relied on or were assisted by other people, and the moments when you bravely took a punt on something yourself. It should give you the confidence to do either of those things again.

People often say that a chief executive's office can be a lonely place, and in some respects it is. The buck stops with you. Your decision is final. Your name is on the headline when things go either very right, or very wrong.

But it depends on your attitude towards seeking counsel from others. You can always learn from people who know much more about their specific area than you do. (Remember that chat we had about generalists in a specialist world?)

People on the front line – who haven't had to be promoted out of a public-facing role! – will have priceless intelligence to impart, however many steps down the staircase they may be.

Discussions like these can often be the trigger for creating opportunities that didn't exist before, and as a senior manager that's really exciting stuff. It's the incentive that should be getting you out of bed in a morning.

Who knows what can happen when you have conversations with people? If you approach things with an open mind, you may stumble upon a nugget of gold. And the productivity can be reciprocal.

Most people, I find, are very open to having those kinds of conversations. Sometimes they are flattered that you want to listen to their opinion in the first place.

Swiss psychiatrist Carl Jung said: "Everything that irritates us about others can lead us to an understanding of ourselves."

Wise words. Although I'm not saying it's a completely foolproof philosophy . . . it's important to accept that there's always going to be half a per cent of the people you meet who you'll be perfectly justified to just write off as a complete and utter waste of time. I refer you back to Rule Seven!

If Covid has done anything, though, it is to prove to us that there are more ways than we think to get from position A to position B. Who says we have to drive to a face-to-face meeting? Who says we need to wear a shirt and tie for a board meeting? Who says we need to work nine-to-five with an hour off for lunch?

We can be masters and mistresses of our own destinies, to a much greater degree than we think.

There's a slightly cryptic saying in business: 'Don't waste a good crisis'. Some people associate it with the days of Winston Churchill, but it was in fact uttered by a chief of staff in the office of former US president Barack Obama during the global credit crunch of 2007 and 2008.

He told a Wall Street Journal forum: "You never want a serious crisis to go to waste.

And what I mean by that is, it's an opportunity to do things you think you could not do before."

Strategies that would have otherwise been unpalatable or unthinkable are suddenly on the table. You find yourself questioning far more about life's rules and regulations.

I think that in years to come, with the passage of time, we will come to view the Covid years as akin to other cataclysmic global events like Spanish Flu, or World War Two – so profound.

When people ask me about my approach to handling the pressure of leadership, I always tell them that the secret is to keep pedalling, and don't look down! Why? Because both of those actions are driven by a fear of falling over…

Maybe that's a slightly glib response, but it's my shoot-from-the-hip comment if people ever ask me how I do things. I believe there's a lot of truth in it, but I'm also acutely aware that it's not great when you're writing a book about leadership to suggest that the secret of success is to just close your eyes, move quickly and hope for the best!

The point is to make sure that you don't pedal fast and be stupid. When a youngster is being taught to ride their bike, they're often told not to think about it too much, aren't they? That's because they'll fall off if they do.

You can always find a reason for not doing something if you dwell for long enough. And that's a recipe for paralysis and inefficiency. Managing your stress levels, and keeping yourself on an emotionally even keel as much as possible, is something which must never be overlooked.

The biggest emotion I tend to feel is frustration, rather than any degree of anger, elation or upset. That's because I know what I want to see happening, I'm trying my best to get there and bring everyone with me, but I don't always feel like I get there fast enough.

People aren't always immediately on your wavelength. They sometimes need time to process what you are asking, and get into the right mind space themselves. But if they get there eventually, that's OK isn't it?

People say to me: "Running a local authority, you must be in a constant state of stress?"

I wouldn't describe it as stress. The definition of stress, for me, is something which is out of control, and I rarely feel chaotic or out of control. Yes, I can get frustrated about things which I'd like to see changed, which are beyond my sphere of influence, but that's different.

I take a leaf out of Emmy and Golden Globe-winning actor Martin Sheen's book. He famously said: "Only fight the fights you can win. Fight the fights that need fighting!"

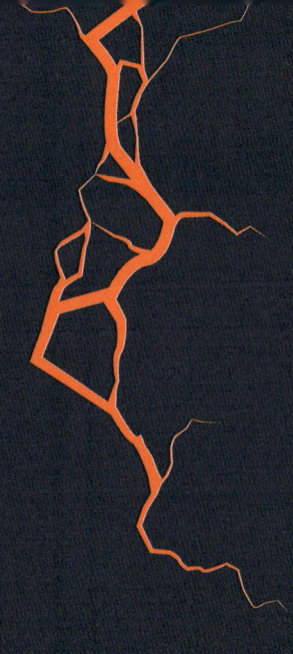

"We have had a number of devastating setbacks; how these are handled is the making of a great team ... winning does not happen in straight lines."

Sir Clive Woodward

CHAPTER *seven*

B-class C-suites?

Have you ever sat down and compared yourself to a teabag? If not, you really should try it some time.

You don't need to be a connoisseur of a nicely-brewed cuppa; the principles are sound either way. I look at it like this. Some tea bags come with premium labels, huge TV advertising budgets and bold, psychedelic packaging. Others are built on a more discreet, no-nonsense brand strategy.

None of this peripheral stuff is really important though. The only thing that matters is how the tiny little tea bag inside that box performs when it's plunged into boiling hot water.

Just like the true character of a person who is placed into a pressurised business environment, this is the moment when they show their true colours.

People can talk a good game, dress in the sharpest of suits, and be blessed with the gift of the gab, but it's how they behave when they find themselves in 'hot water' that really matters. Which is where the teabag analogy comes into its own.

Remember, the quality of the drink is determined by how the tea inside the bag performs when the heat is on, not by the label, string or advertising campaign. Your key staff can be viewed in the same way.

I like 'tea bags' who are just chomping at the bit for the chance to throw themselves head-first into that vat of boiling water. They don't see it as a risk of dissolving and disintegrating, but as an opportunity to show what they are really made of.

The best managers will be able to spot these people, and give them sufficient time to 'brew'. Because just as a cup of tea isn't ready to drink the moment the bag is dipped into hot water, corporate 'tea bags' need some time to acclimatise and assess the atmosphere and their surroundings when the heat is on.

If you're lucky enough to have these brave, committed 'tea bags' in your organisation, nurture, cherish, challenge and reward them, because I'm increasingly of the opinion that the bar is being lowered almost universally in every walk of life these days.

I know that's a horrible thing to say (maybe it has something to do with my age), but it feels like accepted standards have been dumbed down in recent years.

Things which never used to be acceptable are no longer even questioned as anomalies, and it manifests itself in some of the conversations and individuals I see and hear among bosses in those so-called C-suite positions.

I'm referring to top senior executives whose titles tend to start with the letter C, like chief executive, chief financial officer, chief operating officer, and chief information officer. People in powerful, responsible, highly-paid and influential positions.

> **Frankly, I wouldn't give some of these people the remote control to my TV set, never mind the directorship of a multi-million-pound organisation. It's terrifying.**

I don't understand how we've got to a place where this is acceptable; where owners of businesses across multiple sectors are simply saying 'well, that's just how it is these days' and letting it pass by unchecked.

No it's not. Why can't we push back against this and lift that bar higher for everyone's benefit?

I'm not satisfied with running a good organisation, or one that is just stable, safe or treading water. I want to be part of an excellent, top-performing organisation that is constantly striving to do better.

I want to keep pushing those individuals that are in my C-suite to be the best they can absolutely be, and that means addressing all of our shortfalls and constantly re-assessing, looking for the next development opportunity, and questioning whether our standards and practices could be higher, more efficient, or just simply better.

It's about always looking to self-critique, review and compare – against whatever your organisation's measures of success or failure happen to be. At the very least, any self-respecting leader should have the discipline and genuine commitment to aspire to that.

Are we no longer in a world where it is deemed appropriate, or possible, for a manager to call a halt to proceedings and say 'that's simply not acceptable – if you are going to hold down this position we require a certain quality of decision-making approach'? Sometimes I wonder.

My thoughts drift back to Sir Clive Woodward here, who used the T—CUP theory to such powerful effect. Thinking Clearly Under Pressure.

Understanding how your team is performing, what is working particularly well, what needs improvement, and what being an exceptional team really looks like.

Sir Clive is one of my heroes, and I've been lucky enough to meet and share inspirational conversations with him in recent times.

Perhaps we are just reaping the harvest of what we have sown socially over the past few decades, where there is now a whole generation of people who have been either over-indulged, and never been told the word 'no' in a tone which makes it crystal clear it is not up for debate.

There is so much which is great about Generation Alpha and Generation Z – they are some of the most educated and independent people on our planet. But at risk of coming across sounding like a grumpy old man and making sweeping generalisations, they do also come with an awful lot of challenges as well.

For them, growing up's not that complex at all – it's just about Googling stuff and living life in a virtual world. Ask them to make a phone call or strike up some chit-chat by walking into a room full of strangers though, and that can be a different matter altogether. Unlike the older generation, it's not been their world. They have many other virtues, though – many far beyond the reach of even the most aspirational of us 'oldies'.

Technology is undoubtedly making many parts of our lives swifter and more efficient, but it's also contributing to the loss of some of the personal nuances and capabilities of engaging in conversation which remain – and should always be – a pivotal part of our working lives.

There are many new world issues that we all have to deal with, but for me, this goes back to the very essence of my motivation for writing this book – not losing sight of the fact that the fundamentals of good leadership are built on common sense.

There is no silver bullet, no magic wand, no AI program that's going to do it all for you. It's about you taking the responsibility and initiative, and breaking down any given challenge to work out how you can best solve the problem.

That's why, for all the changes we are living through in our increasingly chaotic world, I make no apology for continuing to be scathing about sub-standard attitudes or behaviours among C-suites.

The dangerous bit is that often, these people feel that their position is an automatic endorsement of their capability and competence. It quite obviously isn't.

One of the great dilemmas for a leader is just how far ahead you should be planning. A year, five years, a decade? Some of the tools you may be using in ten years' time might not even have been invented yet!

Few people actually want to position themselves right at what they call the 'bleeding edge' of development.

If you do, you are a guinea pig for a product or service that's so new and experimental it probably hasn't yet been fully tested, and may turn out to be flawed or unreliable.

The result: you'll be experiencing design troubles and bugs that hadn't been foreseen by the developers – and your competitors will be only too pleased to sit back and let you make all the mistakes for them to seize upon and learn from.

It's why lots of people want to be tucked away in the middle of the developmental pack, which is seen as the safest place. Personally, I like being at that vanguard, putting fresh footprints in the sand.

As a local government chief executive, I'm constantly asking myself how I can work with other sectors, with the public sector, private sector, governments of other countries, academics and industry leaders all over the globe, on issues of common interest.

The secret lies in creating conditions for success. Creating that fertile ground.

I don't know what opportunities may be round the corner, in the same way as not knowing that training harder on a Thursday night would lead to me scoring more tries on a Saturday.

But I have no other basis to recommend this than my own experience which says; the more you do this, the better the opportunities are that seem to come your way. That's as deeply as I can dissect this.

My sense is that opportunities are within my grasp, and that I need to simply create the conditions to open up dialogue for collaborations which could lead to success. Pushing forward, trying new things, challenging the norm, and asking questions.

Do I know what this is going to end up looking like? Absolutely not. But I have a strategy to get to – what I'm convinced is – some very fertile ground.

The evolution of social media in recent times is a good case in point here. Take Linkedin, for example. For years it was a very binary platform for essentially sharing your CV and skill-set – a Facebook for grown-ups, they used to say.

But how does it actually leverage all of the information which people are trying to share, so that I, the user, get to have the right kind of conversations with people all over the world for a mutually beneficial, collaborative discussion around shared interests?

Just because I work for local government doesn't mean I only want to network with others in my sector. Agricultural industries don't just want to speak with farmers. Actors don't just want to speak to luvvies. We have to open our minds.

Decision-making takes courage, involves identifying and seizing the chances when they come along . . . and, of course, there's a bit of luck involved along the way too!

"Never confuse movement with action."
Ernest Hemingway

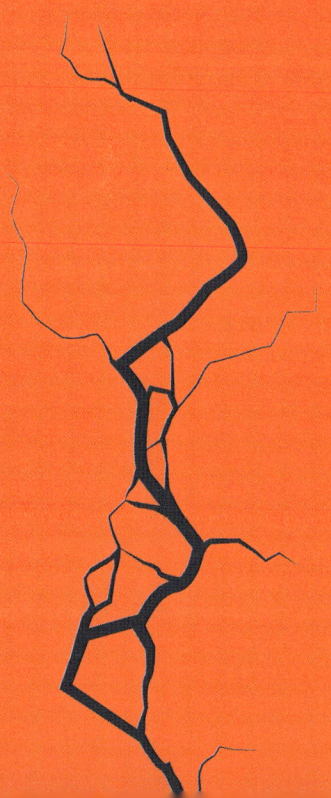

CHAPTER *eight*

Confidence tricks & boardroom aikido

What is it they say? You don't get a second chance to make a first impression.

Projecting the wrong kind of image for your organisation can damage the currency of your brand, not to mention damaging the motivation of your workforce.

Get it right, on the other hand, and it can inject some real energy, excitement and momentum, making you and your team believe that anything is possible.

It was ancient philosopher Aristotle who first offered the suggestion that a person could become virtuous if they acted virtuously.

Fast forward to the 1970s, and this was translated into the slogan 'Fake it 'til you make it'.

However you want to couch it, it's certainly the starting point for a very interesting and important debate.

The idea that by imitating confidence, competence, and applying an optimistic mindset, you can load the dice more heavily in your favour and improve your chances of success.

I'm not so sure about the 'faking it' bit – but I do see the value of spending time doing a spot of window dressing to ensure you are looking fresh, reliable and relevant.

As a leader, you'll have a vision of where you want your organisation to go. That journey could be a long and difficult one, so it's imperative that you take your disciples with you along the way.

To achieve this, you'll need to instil confidence and belief, and some of this could well call for a spot of window dressing – putting a glossy spin on your plans.

Not just for the benefit of your staff, but for customers too. Would you take your shiny car to be serviced at a rusting, run-down tin shed of an operation with a 'for sale' board outside, or choose the welcoming, well-groomed rival down the road whose premises are clean and shiny?

I'm not saying you should 'fake it' – in my experience people see through hollow or unfounded promises more quickly than ever these days – but if you don't give the impression of someone who believes you will reach your goal, you probably won't, because your staff will sense the uncertainty and insecurity and vote with their feet.

If your team members believe you can win, on the other hand, they will raise their game to perform better. And so will you.

When I first took on the chief executive's role at Shropshire Council, I was asked what I felt needed to be injected into the organisation the most. My answer was belief.

If our 3,500 staff believe the authority can change, operate in a different way, be resilient, and if they are freed up to do the job they came in to do, they will be right behind you and give everything.

That's what I believe people naturally want to do when they come to work, so it's not as much of an uphill struggle as you might think.

Window dressing can only get you so far, of course; you have to have a sound business plan on firm foundations built behind those curtains. The warning signs for a prospective customer will come when they want to venture behind that snazzy frontage to find out what makes an organisation tick, but find they can't get through the front door.

Has this organisation got something to hide? Are they all mouth and no trousers? That's what they will come to think.

Remember, it's very easy to design an all-singing online shop window these days which can make you look like a heavy-hitting international company, when you're actually just one person working on a laptop in your spare bedroom. Faking it and hoping you are going to make it.

Every business has to start somewhere, of course, and I'm not for a moment knocking those who create a fantastic online presence for their start-up. All I'm saying is that it's important to recognise that there will be some businesses out there which spend a disproportionate amount of time on their window dressing, at the expense of strategy or indeed customer service.

> **If you look slick and professional, you're raising people's expectations, so you have to make damned sure you meet or ideally exceed them.**

Being able to describe yourself as an award-winning business does no harm either. I'm a firm believer in the benefits of taking part in competitions to test yourself against your peers.

Having a trophy in the cabinet, or a certificate on the wall, is just another way to make your staff walk that little bit taller, proud in the knowledge they have played a part in your success.

So you've built an attractive shop window and enticed the customer inside, eager to find out more. What now? My starting point is to always be up front, open and honest.

Which is just as well, because I make a terrible liar – my memory's not good enough to recall what I've said, and to whom, or to be trying to play mind games. So I play things with a straight bat.

I'm a firm believer that, in the long run, honesty never fails. It can be uncomfortable in the short term sometimes because you may have to tell people things they don't want to hear, admit to your own mistakes, or paint a picture of your organisation's situation that will involve delivering some harsh home truths.

But the majority of your colleagues will appreciate the honesty. Why make things up, or do that classic soap opera trick of dragging a storyline out for weeks by avoiding having the conversation you know needs to take place? I just don't get it.

Most people value the truth far more than you may imagine. Sometimes, in fact, you'll find they've already worked it out for themselves and are just waiting for you to be up front and open with them.

By not shying away from the difficult issues, I think you can gain a great deal of respect as a leader and build a really strong bond with colleagues. It also means you carry around far less mental baggage.

> **When it comes to tackling those tricky scenarios, I often utilise what I call 'boardroom Aikido'.**

I'm not talking about practising martial arts in the office, but taking a leaf out of its founding philosophy.

Roughly translated, Aikido is 'the way of harmonious spirit', and was founded on a goal of overcoming tension without the use of violent or aggressive acts.

In a boardroom scenario, this manifests itself as using your opponent's strength and speed against them; subtle movements harnessing the impetus of an opponent to steer things in your direction, using their energy as a force for your good.

It's worked for me many times over the years, and proves that you don't have to go toe-to-toe with an opponent, shouting and bawling and being the aggressor.

Stay calm, in the moment, and consider what it is that you are trying to achieve, then reflect on why it is that your opponent is behaving in this way. Harness the energy and movement they are creating to turn it into your direction of travel.

Remember what I was saying earlier about knowing when it's time to listen, rather than speak?

A mindset like this allows you to recognise drivers and triggers in people's behaviour, and helps you to metaphorically defend yourself in a respectful way during a boardroom debate – a way which is far less likely to damage corporate relationships, but can still 'floor' your opponent when required.

Part of this process involves taking the time to understand those people who hold opposing views to your own. They're utterly committed, just like you, so if there is a way to somehow harness their energy and enthusiasm – however hard this may be to achieve – it can reap big rewards.

Boardroom Aikido is certainly not the only tool in my box, but it has been a powerful choice on several occasions. It's a case of having the nous to know how and when to engage.

Adaptive leadership is often about knowing which short-cuts to take, and when to take them. There will be occasions when you recognise that you're not doing it properly . . . because you've not got time.

When it comes to making key decisions, I'll bet you've had people tell you: "Follow your gut instinct, it's usually right." It is, and I believe there's a very logical reason for this.

Your body isn't being consumed by some sort of strange supernatural phenomenon; it's making an invisible mental calculation based on your many years of life experiences.

It's silently assessing the people, scenarios and conversations consigned to your memory banks, the consequences which followed, and crunching it all into an algorithm to deliver a 'yes' or 'no' voice in your subconscious.

I don't like being blind-sided by surprises, but I hope no-one would refer to me as a control freak. I like to be in control of the situation, which is a very different thing.

Being prepared is pivotal to this. Sports people will train and practice not to the point where they get it right – but to the stage where their muscle memory means they simply can't get it wrong.

Business is the same. If you've thoroughly rehearsed what you might do in any particularly pressurised situation, it won't be a shock when it comes along.

You'll make your move with confidence, clarity of thought, and be much more decisive.

Pick your emotional battles carefully. Don't get dragged into trying to rationalise or influence elements of your life that you can't control.

Reconcile the fact that these things are going to happen anyway, and don't get wound up about it.

Just shut up, and move on.

Best-selling author Paul McGee has written an excellent book on this subject, called S.U.M.O (Shut Up, Move On).

It explores the importance of taking responsibility for your own life and not being a victim, changing your thinking to change your results, and understanding how to bounce back from setbacks which we all have from time to time.

Increasing your understanding of other people's worlds, and looking at problems and challenges from their perspective, is a good place to start.

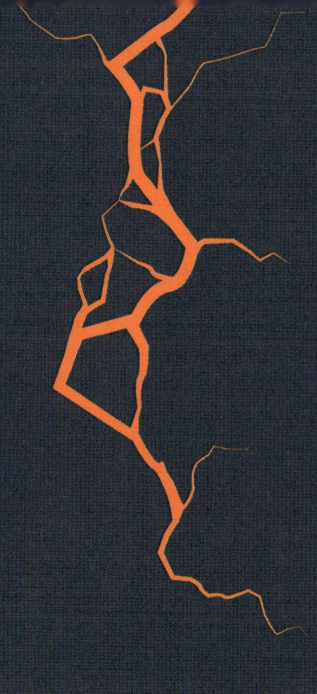

"Listen with curiosity. Speak with honesty. Act with integrity. The greatest problem with communication is we don't listen to understand. We listen to reply."

Roy T. Bennett

CHAPTER *nine*

Data is not a f*cking fossil fuel

Having spoken about the importance of a powerful soundbite, this one really pisses me off.

People keep saying that data is the new oil. I'm sorry, but it's not – it's far, far more powerful. And I'll tell you why.

Let me be openly tactical with you for a minute first. Having said that soundbites are important, that doesn't mean you shouldn't challenge them.

This one, for example, gives you a completely distorted opinion of the truth.

Oil burns brightly when first used, but then its value and power is quickly diminished.

Not so with data, which can be used over and over again, and actually increases in value and power every time you touch it.

Unlike fossil fuel, which is the complete opposite.

Once you understand that, it opens up a wealth of opportunities. There isn't another commodity out there which grows in value in this way, and frankly we're not even scratching the surface yet.

This is another of those scenarios where the crystal ball isn't showing me the full range of opportunities it is going to create – but I know that it's the secret to success, and that I must be alive to the possibilities.

I'd describe myself as having an enthusiastic amateur approach to data – I'm aware of where it has worked effectively to date and can follow the upward curve to appreciate how its influence is only going to grow.

Have you ever found yourself bamboozled by a huge pile of reports and statistics, with no apparently correlating factors?

Chances are that's simply because you're not asking the right questions, or simply don't know what questions you should be asking.

If you look at it through an open mind, a lot of services in the public sector are based on the principle that we respond and deal with crisis and chaos and are really good at helping people out at this time.

My argument is the majority of these instances need not be so chaotic, because they are entirely predictable. It's just we are not wired up to think that way.

Ask yourself, why do American health insurance companies use data analysis to such great effect – because it is commoditised. They know when I'm most likely to have a stroke or heart attack, to an astonishingly accurate degree. As a result, they're far better prepared for peaks in demand.

Staying on the other side of the Atlantic, American retailer Target reportedly discovered that a teenager was pregnant before she knew herself – purely on the back of her changing shopping habits.

It shows just how 'Big Data' can be used to learn pretty much anything about us. It's often said that the Facebooks and Googles of this world seem to know more about our interests than our own family members these days, based on the 'suggested' or 'sponsored' product ads that appear in our timelines.

The world is strewn with these examples. Why do Tesco make so many burgers on any given Saturday in summer? They extrapolate the weather forecast with the time of year, cost of living pressures and opening hours.

Do you manage your stock or resources in this way? If not, why not? It seems to me that we're just not savvy enough to look at what we can learn from all of this valuable data.

> **We don't even recognise that some of our assets actually constitute valuable pieces of data. If only we took the time to join more of the dots together...**

There are other culprits too. Sometimes, people hide behind GDPR and other myths and legends about data sharing for sitting on their hands and doing nothing, but I'm telling you, this stuff is gold dust.

With it, you can prevent everything from sickness to national economic downturns; a million and one different things. It's all there, in front of our noses, right now.

Let me tell you my 'Finding Dave' story that I teased a little bit earlier. It began when our local authority secured funding to carry out a thermal imaging sweep of the county, scanning houses to find which ones were insulated, and which were not.

It was a significant undertaking, but once we'd gathered the information it just sat there on a database doing very little. We must be able to put this to a more nuanced use, I thought.

What other information had we got which could dovetail with it? How about looking at how old people in these houses were, and whether or not they were living alone – information readily available to a council.

Suddenly a scenario emerged where we may be able to help reduce or avoid hospital admissions.

How? By pinpointing people over the age of 80, who lived alone, in a thermally inefficient house. Chances are these people would be staying in one room, by the fire, not getting up to exercise very often or keeping hydrated properly. They were more likely to trip and fall, and highly likely to develop a urinary tract infection.

We calculated that, based on these three lines of data, these people had an 80% chance of turning up at accident and emergency before the end of the year. Clinicians – who won't often put their name to conjecture unless it has near watertight accuracy – said they could believe this, and agreed with the logic.

So we took it a step further. The fire and rescue service needed to know which people to call on for wellbeing visits, and we had the answer staring right at us.

We gave them the list, asked them if they would check for slip and trip hazards while assessing their smoke detection systems, and letting us know if they felt the occupants were socially isolated. We could then come in and support them with emergency heating or potential grants for insulation.

Now, their chance of turning up at accident and emergency had fallen to 20%.

That's three lines of data, reducing chances of hospital admissions for a vulnerable section of society by an incredible 60%. I presented this story at Westminster and summed it up in my final slide by saying: To cut to the chase, it's simply about finding Dave before Dave finds us.

When I came off the stage, a woman came up to me and said: "I loved your Finding Dave campaign" – which at that point it never actually was. Subsequently, it gained legs, and now there is an entire workstream at the council called Finding Dave. If the woman in question is reading this, drop me a line and we can discuss royalties!

Joking aside, let's remember that all this came from thinking laterally about just three lines of data which was already in our grasp.

What I find incredibly frustrating is that so many of us are in possession of these kind of datasets, and the capability of doing incredible things with them, but the potential is just not being fulfilled.

> **Imagine if you are sitting on not three, but three hundred lines of data. Or even three thousand? The possible game-changing benefits are mind-boggling.**

Those companies which have seen the light are the ones which are flying. Amazon tells me what I want to buy – not by some strange coincidence, but because it recognises the power of data, and knows how to use it. Their algorithms are incredibly accurate.

It takes a significant amount of nerve for a chief executive, in times of crisis or financial stress, to take a decision not to firefight specific issues by targeting resources at a problem – and instead divert those resources into more in-depth strategic data analytics which will automatically be helping to predict these things for us in the first place.

That can be a very tough thing to sell to your stakeholders, particularly if they've not yet made that quantum leap into the same mindset. People have to find their own ways of opening their eyes to how the use of Big Data can revolutionise their products and processes. But they need to do it sooner rather than later.

We talked earlier about your gut instinct when it comes to decision making, and how more often than not it'll be the right call.

But what if your gut is telling you one thing, and the data is saying something completely different?

In a situation like this, you have got to ask yourself whether you have really experienced enough in your life to compare like-for-like with what the data set has extrapolated. This may be a case of your gut being less accurate than an infinite number of different data sets – hard as that could be to 'stomach'.

Or indeed this could be the perfect time to test your gut instinct . . . keeping an open mind to the results.

Remember, these two things do not have to be mutually exclusive. You can test your gut feeling in a controlled situation, with the safety of the data on hard drive. It means you can ask questions in a controlled setting without there needing to be catastrophic consequences.

We also talked earlier about the role played by futurologists, thought leadership and the fifth industrial revolution, which is making use of all the data then re-introducing emotion into the system.

This is an example where it can come to the fore. The question we should be asking is what can we, as humans, add to the equation once the data has been worked up for us?

Our thoughts, emotions and values remain really important in this space, and should never be underestimated.

I can't pore over 10,000 different spreadsheets looking for a few common denominators or trends, but AI can. My role as a senior leader, which is much more valuable and time-efficient, is to focus on asking it the right questions, and telling it what to look for.

Get it right, and that equates to extra pounds, shillings and pence in your business really quickly.

The young generation are so comfortable interacting with all this data; they've never known a world where it didn't exist in such useable form.

But whatever your age or demographic, I believe that once you have seen the results of what it can do in a small way, you can extrapolate that really quickly and find your eyes being opened to its almost infinite potential.

People are naturally resistant to change. There are those who feel AI and the world of Big Data is a direct threat to their jobs.

I would say it's not a threat to your job, if you are prepared to embrace the fact that it means you will have to do your job differently.

Those who look at it with a glass half-full mentality, and ask how it can help them to do their jobs, are the ones who will be happiest, and most successful in the future that lies before us.

Most of the time, automation is going to be perfect for tackling the sort of repetitive, tedious tasks that we don't particularly enjoy anyway. Think of the time that will free up for you to explore some more creative, outside-the-box ideas, using your brain, your emotion, and your intuition.

Let me ask you this: what is it that you do in your job that adds value for the business? It's a self-reflection and self-development question that everyone would do well to consider.

As a board of directors, or as individuals, what are you bringing to the party that no-one else can do, and everyone else needs? Are you thinking creatively, or just rubber-stamping other people's work?

If the explosion of data has done anything, it's to implore us to re-assess the roles of our senior leaders far more frequently.

If you have a place in the strategic leadership team, then lead strategically, and don't waste time checking other people's homework. Let's allow the world of data to move us away from traditional constructs.

Real leadership should be courageous and meet some of these challenges head-on, as well as safeguarding the creative, supporting and nurturing aspects which remain so vital in the role.

So what am I really saying here? Using the data at your fingertips correctly will radically shift your operating model, and I don't think people have switched on to this fast enough yet.

> **The fourth industrial revolution is all about the capabilities of AI and how we understand and use the incredible array of tools it provides to us.**

But futurologists tell us that the fifth industrial revolution is a far more interesting and influential one – because it's the time when we'll take the best bits of AI and technology, but reintroduce emotion and feeling back into the system.

That may sound a bit nebulous, but it's our own humanity which must always be the spark.

Should we reconfigure the working day, working week, or calendar year – these are Victorian values after all which we need not necessarily be wedded to. Why work 9-5 Monday to Friday? Do we need specified weekends, or a set number of annual holidays?

The really exciting bit for me is that the power of Big Data has accelerated this thinking and, in many instances, persuaded us to look at rechannelling liability to turn it into a resource.

Take social care as an example, one of my previous career roles. There are critics who only see it as a costly drain on resources where demand constantly outstrips supply.

If you just press pause for a second and think about what it looks like as a system, as a whole, it is actually one of the biggest industries in the UK, contributing significantly to the local and national economy.

Think about the people it employs, the contractors it uses, the people it serves, and flip this all around. Suddenly you are no longer looking at this financial black hole which is draining us dry, but as a resource itself; a driver of the economy. I am pleased to say that my 'Flipping Social Care' narrative is still frequently referred to within the realms of Health and Social Care.

It's a reminder of how you really should examine any given scenario from as many different perspectives as you can. You might be surprised.

The big challenge is to create the conditions where you and your colleagues are actively encouraged to think differently about each of the pieces in your organisational jigsaw. Or better still, compelled to do so.

We also need to admit and recognise that, at the very moment you are reading this, it's already going to be out of date!

That's the nature of this debate. Recognising that reality of the situation is what's pivotal.

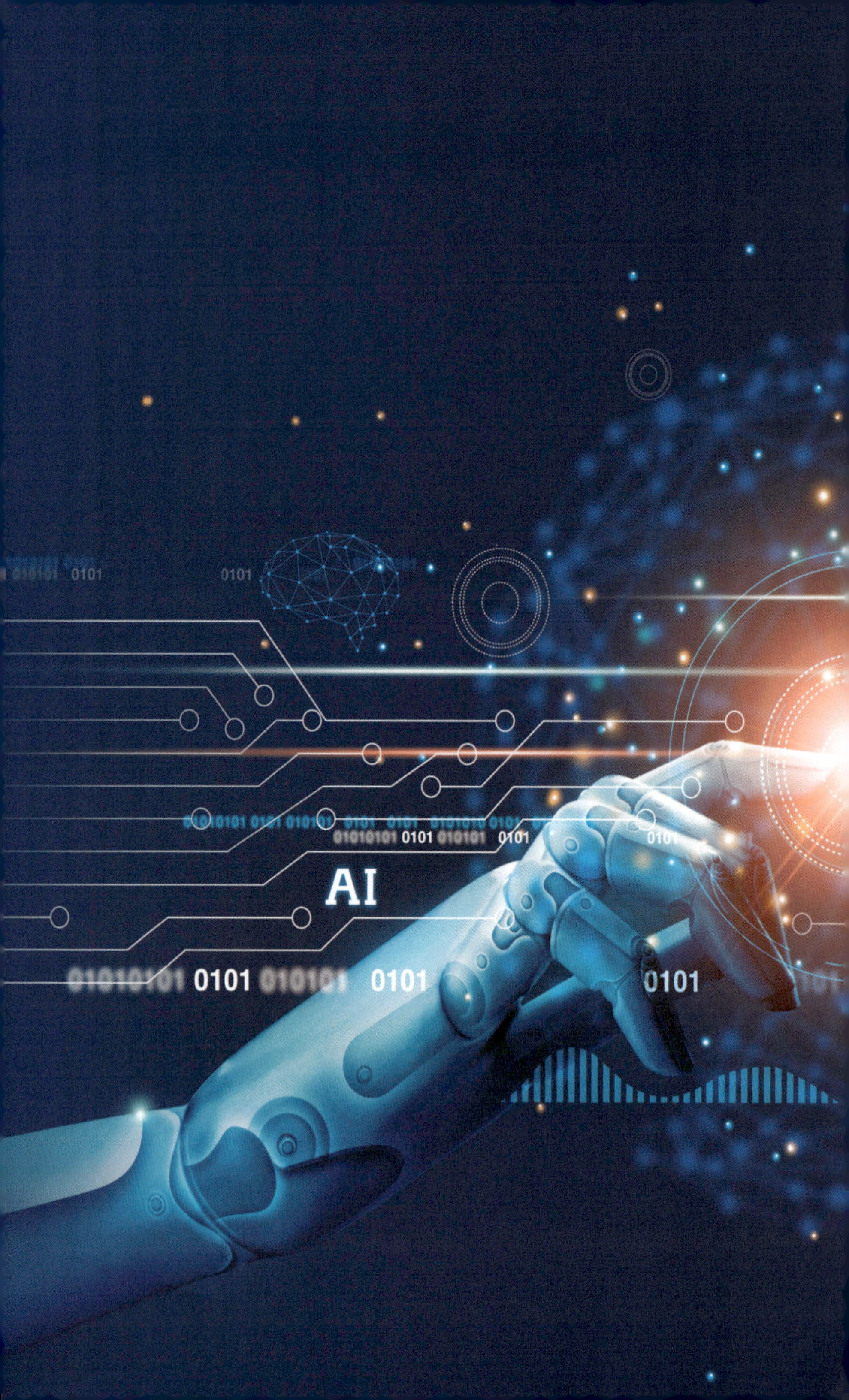
AI
0101 0101 0101

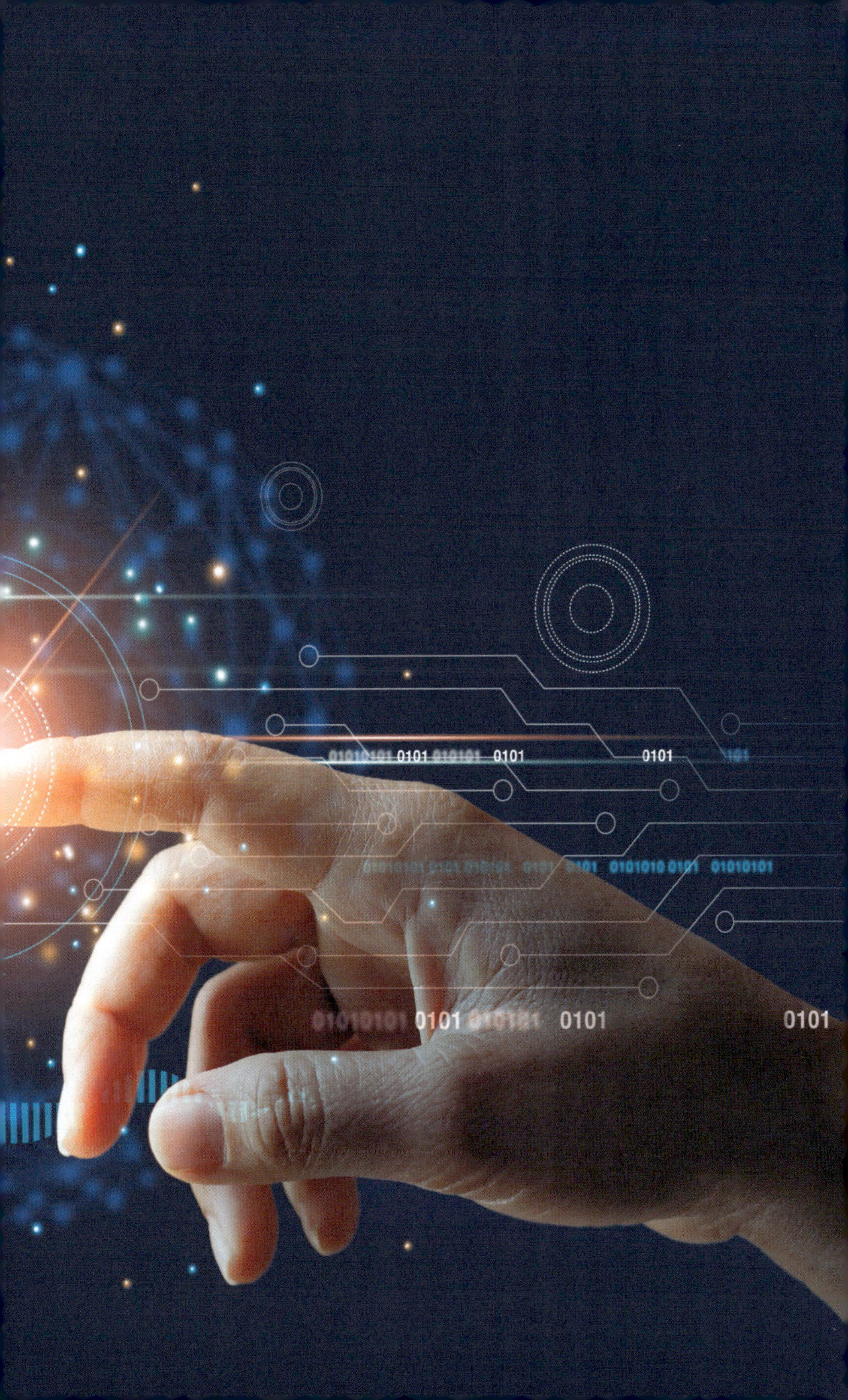
0101
0101
0101
0101
0101
0101

> "*If you can't explain it simply to a six-year-old, you don't understand it well enough.*"
> **Albert Einstein**

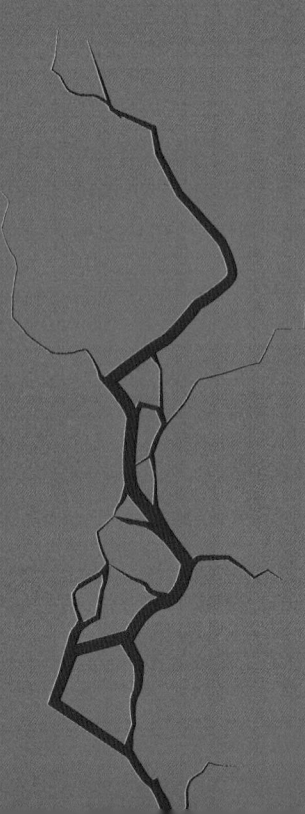

CHAPTER *ten*

The benefits of foresight, and the comfort of not knowing

Sometimes in business, people spend an awful lot of time answering questions which never need to be asked.

I'm reminded of the famous story about the World War Two aviation engineers who spent months trying to work out where best to place armour-plating on aeroplanes to protect them from enemy gunfire.

Their strategy was built around evidence gathered from carefully inspecting bullet-ridden planes which returned from cross-channel missions, and assessing which parts of the fuselage had taken the greatest amount of gunfire.

They'd count up the bullet holes, and plan to place extra armour in the areas which had attracted the heaviest fire.

Perfectly logical, you'd think . . . except for one vital factor which had been overlooked.

The boffins were only actually basing their evidence on the planes that made it back home safely! What about all the others which were shot down by German anti-aircraft fire?

Suddenly, it dawned on them that they had been mapping precisely the wrong thing.

It was Hungarian-born mathematician Abraham Wald who made the game-changing statement that, if a plane had got back to base safely in spite of having its wings riddled by bullet holes, these holes were actually not that dangerous.

Instead, he argued that the technicians should be armouring up the areas which hadn't been hit – because the planes with holes in these places were almost certainly the ones which never made it home.

> **In the blink of an eye, simply by looking at the root of the same problem from a different perspective, the whole strategy had been turned on its head.**

This is why it's always good to have people looking at your business from lots of different perspectives. This way, you're less likely to be wasting time with the best of intentions solving problems that don't exist, or finding your thought patterns heading off down a flawed and blinkered path.

Thinking about things through different lenses will also broaden and potentially change your mindset. It can be a real eye-opener, too.

I find it startling that some people just don't seem to appreciate the importance of this.

They invest huge amounts of time and effort trying to look at things as they are and how they can make a product or process better, instead of challenging everything from the start – don't fix something you don't need to fix, or which may have become obsolete. Might you not be better off just stopping it altogether and trying something else?

Taking a decision like that can be a difficult pill to swallow, not least to your pride, but it can also separate people that are really successful from those who are not.

> **In today's increasingly volatile, complex, fast-moving and unpredictable world, change is becoming the norm. It's important to embrace it, and not to fear it, and to be among the first to capitalise.**

VUCA is an acronym based on the leadership theories of Warren Bennis and Burt Nanus, to describe and reflect on the Volatility, Uncertainty, Complexity and Ambiguity of conditions and situations.

The United States Army War College used it to help stress-test their policies in the months following the September 11th terrorist attacks in 2001, when military planners were growing increasingly worried about the radically different and unfamiliar international security environment that had emerged in the wake of the World Trade Center's demise.

The VUCA principle is never more relevant than at a time when we are seeing things we never dreamed of, and are having to adapt to them. There has been no shortage of examples in recent years, from the Covid pandemic, to the fourth industrial revolution.

Just as the modern world is an uncertain and, in many ways, unpleasant place, business managers are uncertain, and our team members are uncertain too.

This is where leaders must step up to the plate. We must not be frightened of this unpredictability. We must accept and embrace the peaks and troughs. We must absorb uncertainty. It starts by being grown up enough to accept that all of these things are true.

People are irrational at the best of times, so against a backdrop such as this, you can be certain that their mood swings will be amplified.

They might be feeling particularly pissed off one day and be happy as Larry the next – there's very little you can do about that . . . other than to appreciate that this is where tactics, rather than necessarily strategy, come to the fore.

It brings us back to the importance of applying your effort and resources into things which are really going to make a difference.

In process terms, you want to manage the variation, but from a purely human perspective, you equally have to accept and appreciate that variation is always going to exist.

How do you balance process engineering with people engineering? This is one of the keys.

As I've mentioned before, a process can be working flawlessly – until you insert the irrationality of people into the mix.

Against the backdrop of all these variables, it's also important for a leader to accept that they are not going to be 100% right, 100% of the time. Actually, I'm OK with only getting about 80% of our decision-making right, as long as we are actively making decisions, and as long as we are moving quickly enough to implement them. It is unrealistic to expect a perfect hit-rate.

We're reinforcing some of the ground we've already covered here, but again, I make no apology for repeating this; the difference between a good decision and a bad decision is the mechanics you use to reach it.

You might turn left, you might turn right. As long as you made your choice based on sensible and considered analysis of all the information at your fingertips at the time, no manager worth their title should steam in with the benefit of hindsight and tear you to shreds if it turned out you'd headed in the wrong direction.

It might have turned out to be the wrong decision, but it was based on a logical train of thought. That's not the same as a bad decision. Good managers will always appreciate and understand the difference.

In a fast-paced working environment we can all make wrong calls based on the evidence at any given time; a far worse situation would be paralysis, where you're

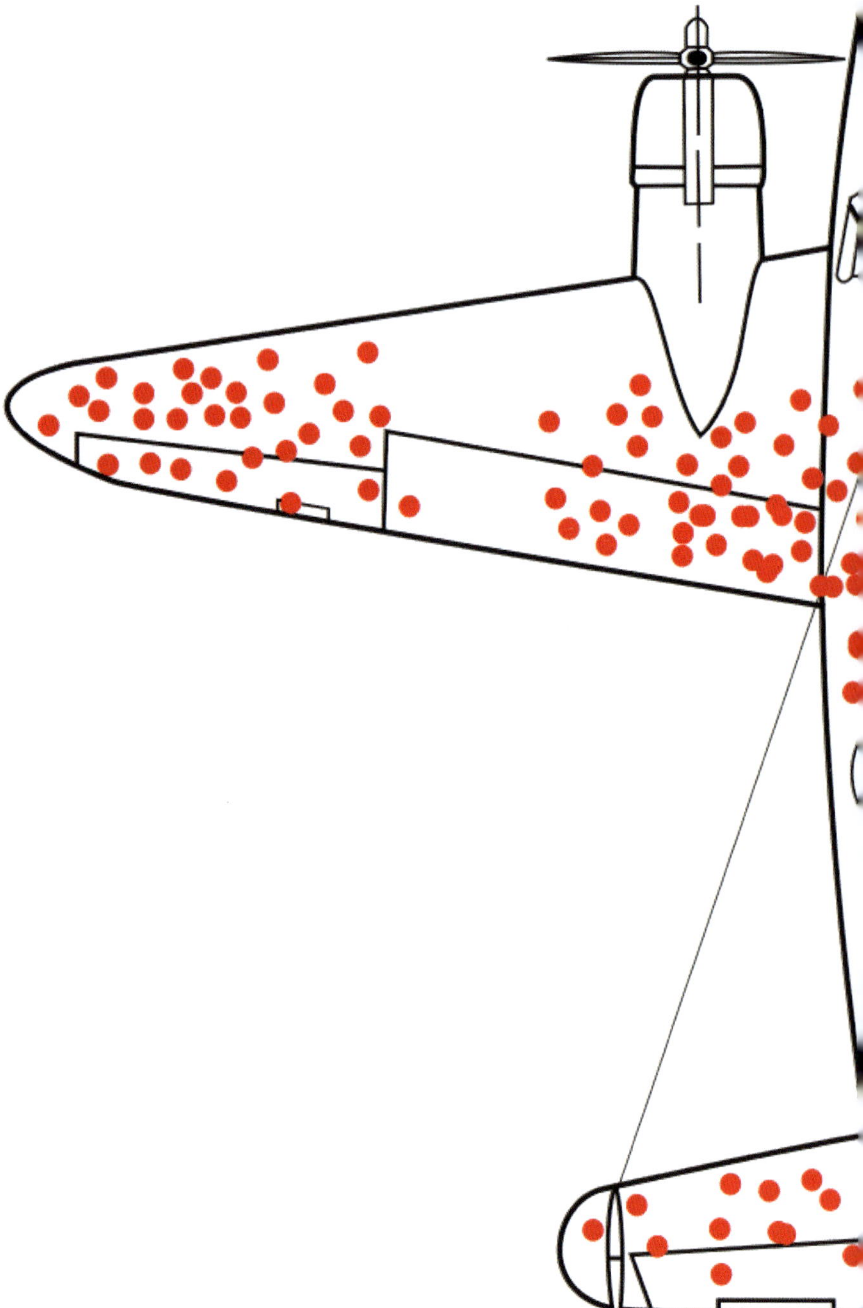

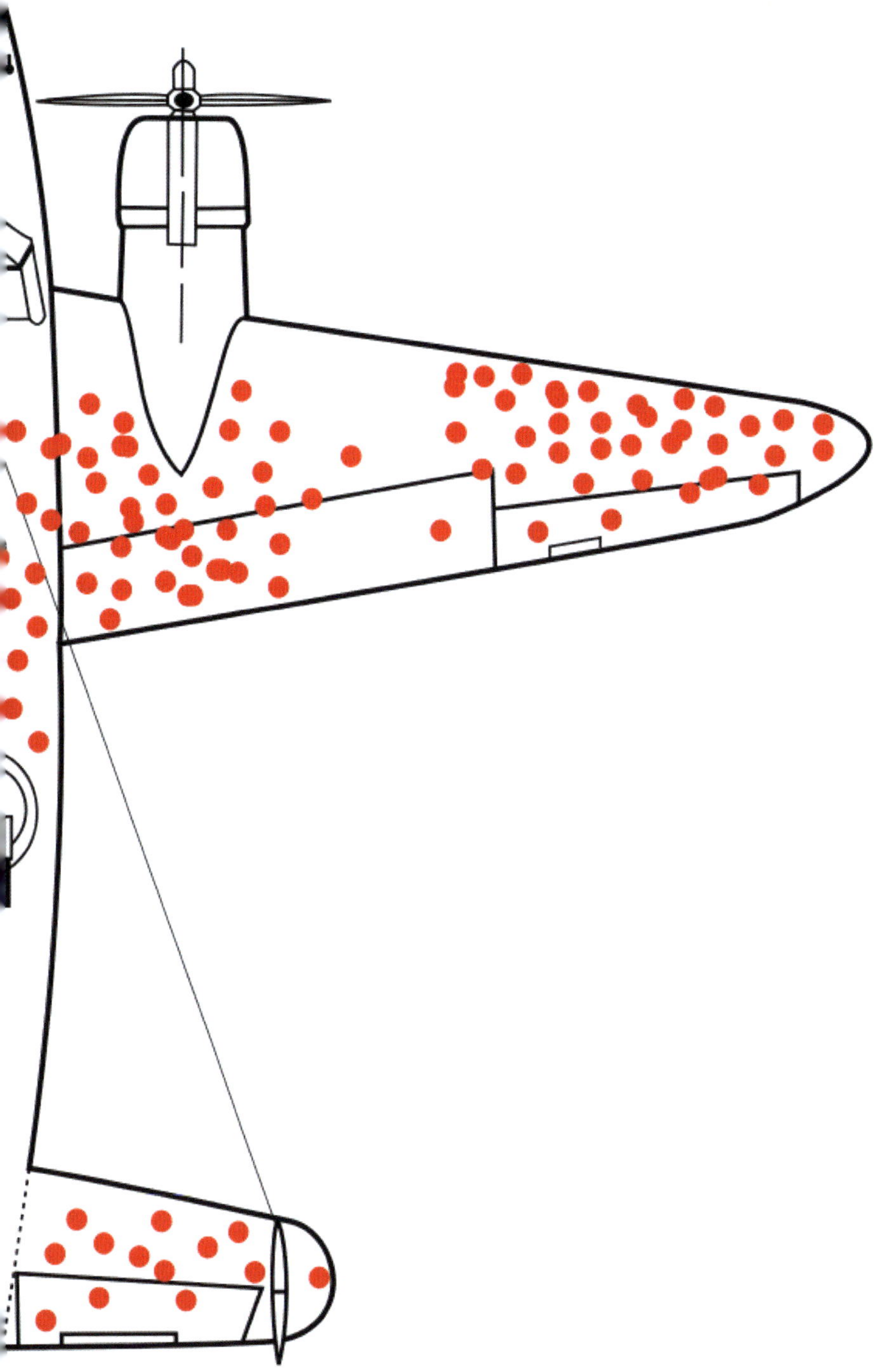

frightened of making a decision at all for fear of the reverberations if it turns out to have been wrong. The roads are littered with indecisive dead squirrels.

And remember I use the word 'wrong' again here, not 'bad'. A bad decision would be deciding to turn left or right merely on a whim, simply because I stuck my finger in the air and thought 'yes, I think that feels right'.

That's tantamount to tossing a coin and leaving your fate to lady luck. This is poor decision-making which, in business, is frankly indefensible. And the harsh reality is the house will always win if you spend enough time in the casino.

If you're going to fail, then the other piece of advice I'd give is to fail fast. Implement a decision (made of course only after careful analysis of the evidence available to you at the time) and if it doesn't work, swallow your pride, move on and don't sit up all night worrying about it. Do something else. Appreciate that you will have learned valuable lessons from the process, so it won't have been a complete waste of time.

As Sir Clive Woodward said: "I never lose, I either win or learn." It's actually a quote he picked up from the late South African leader and regime changer Nelson Mandela.

As long as you have the self-awareness to acknowledge your mistakes, and identify the root cause of them so they are less likely to happen again, you will have added valuable credit to the memory bank and moved forward.

Another phrase you often hear is that you can never live long enough to make all the mistakes yourself. There's an important point here, because what this is really reminding us is that we can also learn from the mistakes of others too.

You have to be pragmatic, and plan for the fact that if you are a bold, ambitious and forward-thinking decision-maker, you will lose sometimes. But the more data you have at your fingertips, the better your odds become.

I've referenced him already but will do so again, because I'm a big fan of author and podcaster Damian Hughes's work. He's written some truly thought-provoking pieces about effective leadership which is relevant across many sectors of business. He tackles the issue of psychological safety, and the principle of BLUF – Bottom Line Up Front.

His view, which I wholeheartedly endorse, is that you will be completely wasting your breath trying to engage with someone, or encouraging them to learn or absorb information, unless that person believes they are both psychologically and physically safe at the time.

In other words, are they in the best possible environment to allow them to blossom and thrive?

It takes us back to that story I referenced earlier about the Kronk gym in the USA –

helping to explain why it was succeeding in nurturing a procession of world boxing champions where others had failed.

When it comes to BLUF, we're all busy people these days, and we just want to cut to the chase, don't we?

People dress things up unnecessarily instead of just getting straight to the punchline. Sometimes, it's because they don't actually have the required clarity of thought themselves, lack confidence or are simply trying to blag it.

Journalists are taught to deliver the most important part of a story in the opening paragraph, to make sure they get a reader's attention in the event that they don't read to the end of the story – well, the same principle applies in the world of business.

Ask yourself this: Are you stripping out all the jargon and making your messages as simple and understandable as you can? Or are you still a prime candidate for your colleagues to be playing a game of bullshit bingo behind your back?

> **Keeping things simple is, more often than not, the secret to making things powerful.**

Can you summarise a movie, a book or a play in one short phrase or sentence – without mentioning its name – in a way that will allow people to identify it? If you can, you've successfully cut to the chase.

People have their own views on the value and validity of social media platform X – or Twitter as it used to be known – but one of its most useful facets in those early days is that it was forcing us to get our message across in a maximum of 140 characters. Cutting out all the fluff and getting straight to the point. Great.

Albert Einstein said: "If you can't explain it simply to a six-year-old, you don't understand it well enough."

Don't ever be afraid of bluntly telling people how it is. Then, once you're sure you have got the main point across, you can start to add any embellishments you feel are necessary to bring more nuance to your plans.

You will find that people will thank you for this approach. They want the bottom line, up front – more so now than ever, given our ever-dwindling attention spans and time pressures.

You only have to speak to regular YouTube creators to endorse this. A couple of years ago they would have been spending hours crafting perfectly edited three or four-minute long pieces; now they have come to realise that a short, sharp 30-second piece on the same subject almost always gets many more hits, even if it's a bit rough round the edges.

Less work for more impact – what's not to like about that?

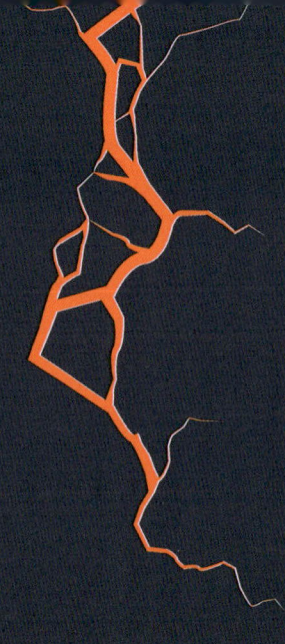

"If you really look closely, most overnight successes took a long time."

Steve Jobs

CHAPTER *eleven*

Evolution doesn't have to be competitive

People often believe evolution has to be a competitive process – we've been programmed to view it as a race to be first, fastest, or best.

But when you look at the data, the only time that evolution actually becomes competitive is – if you forgive the bluntness – when there's fucking or fighting.

The rest of the time it is quite collaborative. Surprisingly so, in fact.

The natural world exists through collaboration and co-operation, and that's all part of our evolution. And yet, we all think of it as an environment where the brightest person, or the most agile person, always wins.

That's simply not true.

Take the story of the Wright brothers, Orville and Wilbur, who wrote their names into the history books as the aviation pioneers who invented, built and flew the world's first successful plane.

What's really interesting here is that, as we neared the end of the 19th century, the American government launched a competition to encourage the invention of powered flight, with an enticing financial incentive on offer.

Thinking it would motivate people to fight for the prize, they sat back and waited.

But the Wright brothers did it differently. They weren't motivated by the government's tactics. Instead of putting on the blinkers and reaching for the pot of gold, they instead reached out to collaborators.

Far from shrouding their experiments and calculations in secrecy, they toured the country and gave talks about their work, as well as writing in a string of respected journals.

As a result, they became the first to achieve a controlled, sustained flight of an engine-powered, heavier-than-air aircraft with the Wright Flyer in December 1903.

Collaboration had trumped competition.

There's an old adage that people don't buy from companies, they buy from people.

How strictly true that is these days in our increasingly faceless online commercial world is open to some doubt.

Actually, I believe that if a particular product or service is of value to you, and competitively priced, a buyer will part with their cash whatever they feel about a salesperson. Or indeed, they'll complete the transaction online without coming close to engaging with a human being at all.

But this should never be used as a reason to overlook the importance of fostering face-to-face business relationships, because you never know where they could lead.

People often don't quite appreciate the value of this investment, because there may not be an immediate or obvious return.

And indeed, unless you are insisting all of your business contacts complete one of those 'How did you hear about us?' questionnaires, you may never actually know how precious your time has been.

Fostering a strong and productive relationship may take a couple of years, but in my experience taking the time and patience to build these foundations will almost always have been worth it.

After all, why would you not want to spend time understanding what matters to your customers and explaining the value you can bring?

In a world which is being increasingly dominated by machine learning and artificial intelligence, humanising your organisation is fast becoming a powerful USP.

We're already seeing major corporations refocusing their advertising to emphasise the fact that, if you ring their call centre, you'll be able to speak to a 'real person' – something which not so many years ago we all took for granted!

AI systems may be getting better at replicating human behaviour, but they're not as smart as many would have you believe, and the signs of a kick-back are already emerging.

Sometimes it's about not rushing in, and not being seen to pressurise a contact for a hard sell.

It's no longer a case of hitting them with a list of products or services you want them to buy like some door-to-door chancer, but flipping it on its head and instead investing the time exploring what it is that they want, and need.

There is no success in business without fostering impactful connections with the right people – and that's not something that can be outsourced to an AI bot. Not yet, anyway.

And if you honestly believe you can learn something from everyone you meet, as we discussed earlier, then why wouldn't you want to invest time and effort into building as many strong relationships as you can?

I genuinely believe this; it's not a mindset I've forced myself to adopt simply to further my business aspirations.

Of course, as we've explored before, there will always be a tiny percentage of total morons that you don't want to deal with, but in general terms you disregard the building and nurturing of relationships at your peril.

I have seen lots of ineffectual leaders – more often than not those B class C suites – who have either forgotten this, or seem to think that once they have reached their lofty position, the rules change and they don't need certain people any more.

What a fatal mistake that is . . . in reality, you actually need these people more than ever when you reach these positions, but for different reasons.

All of this begs an important question: do you have to be a 'people person' to succeed at the highest levels of business?

I believe it can certainly contribute to your success, because it's all tied up with the critical business traits of being an effective communicator with the ability to understand and empathise with your peers.

But that's not the same as being an attention-grabbing extrovert who goes round spewing out soft soundbites and high-fiving colleagues like a demented David Brent.

I like to think of myself as a people person, but there are still times when I feel dreadfully uncomfortable in big social gatherings – particularly when there's an expectation on you to 'work the room'.

That's not my style at all. But it is incredibly important to still place yourself in these scenarios, because you never know where any given conversation might lead.

It's the same as that rugby analogy – the harder you train, the luckier you get.

Well, the greater the number of business arenas you choose to enter, the more likely you are to strike gold with a brilliant and potentially unexpected business contact.

Putting yourself out there, making connections, having those conversations, and listening, can make you look at life through a different lens. Suddenly you can find yourself in a whole different mind space, which certainly keeps me motivated.

We've spoken already about the importance of taking time to consider how you are perceived as a leader, and how this perhaps compares to how you see yourself.

> **It's easy to assume that people know and understand more about you than they actually do. They won't know what's going on in your head, until there is some physical evidence.**

I've ended up having some fascinating and enriching conversations simply by making myself available for debates, or signing up for conferences and seminars which may not be the most obvious choices for a local authority chief executive.

Why do I do this? I take the view that it's essential if you want to reconfigure and redesign the role of the public sector, which I'm of the opinion is precisely what's required.

Current traditional thinking isn't going to get us there; we've got to step out of that, so I'm interested in having global conversations with investors, academics, and thought leaders from all sorts of different sectors with whom I may not have any immediately obvious common ground.

But do you know what? I find they are equally interested in speaking to me too.

They are intrigued to find out why someone from my sector wants to put himself into their thought space. I've put the bait out there by my mere presence, and found they are very keen to strike up a dialogue. Fortuitous? Sometimes. But you've got to be in it to win it.

Who knows where this sort of thing will lead. But that's the point, isn't it?

I've no idea exactly what's going to come of this approach or which direction it will take me, but I know it's not going to have been a waste of my time. Because again, if nothing else I'm accumulating data to squirrel away in my memory banks.

One of the most unexpectedly brilliant spin-offs from this approach came when I was invited, out of the blue, to a thought leadership event being held in Paris, sponsored by French president Emmanuel Macron.

Only a small number of invitations were sent out – but my name was somehow on the list, which was quite mind-blowing in itself to be honest.

Why on earth would a chief executive of a shire county authority in the heart of the UK be on their radar, you might ask?

Well, it was because they were desperate to hear a different perspective on business from a senior leader in the public sector, and nobody had shown any interest in wanting to have those conversations – because, let's face it, local authority chief executives don't tend to mix in those circles, do they?

Many would say: 'Why would we? Why should we? That's not our area of specialism, and is none of our business.' But I disagree with that. I think I have to be as outward-facing as I am inward-facing.

> **We all have to be fleet of foot, agile and adaptive, and we can only do this by stepping outside to take a look at everything on the horizon, from every possible perspective.**

Simply by showing an enthusiasm to participate in, shall we say, less traditional forums, my name had found its way onto the French team's radar, which I took as a real vindication of this approach.

It was also a reminder of just how powerful it can be to put yourself out there, shifting people's expectations, challenging the status quo, and meeting fascinating people with wildly differing backgrounds and skill sets.

Why don't we do something different? Why don't we start alternative conversations? Why don't we surprise people by demonstrating that we are not content to slavishly stick to the rules and regulations of the past?

The globe is shrinking, and we can have meetings online with anybody, anywhere. That's exciting, isn't it?

Why would you not want to explore the opportunities that this could open up?

This gets me out of bed in the morning.

"*Act as if what you do makes a difference. It does.*"

William James

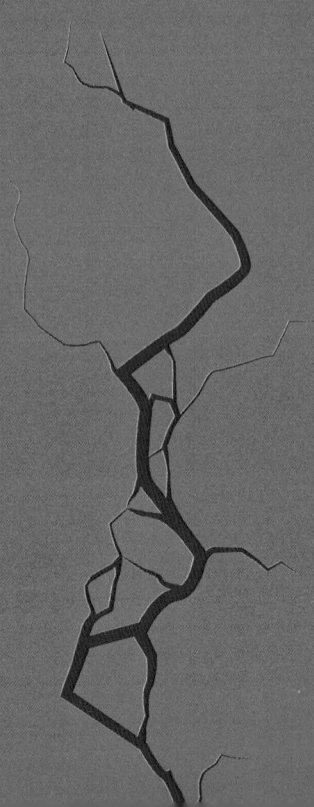

CHAPTER *twelve*

What free words

Your words as a leader cost you nothing, yet they are without doubt the most powerful weapons in your armoury.

As a chief executive of a local authority employing several thousand people, the children of our employees will know my name. I've never met them, but they'll know about me. That's powerful stuff.

So just stop and think about it…. seriously.

All of those people who don't work in my organisation know my name, and would recognise my face. Not just the children of my colleagues, but quite probably a lot of their friends and relatives too.

If that doesn't stop you in your tracks and make you think about the impact of what you say to people, and the tone in which you say it, then it bloody well should!

There's a fascinating book by John Amaechi called The Promises of Giants which is worth checking out on this subject.

It discusses the fact that, in today's increasingly disruptive and perilous world, the need for people with the skill and the will to collaborate has never been greater.

Not only because it makes life better and more pleasurable for everyone, but because it brings more positive results too.

He says: "The most unlikely of people, in the most improbable of circumstances, can become extraordinary."

Amaechi draws on a wealth of experience, from accompanying his mother, a doctor, on her visits to tend to dying patients, to his time as a top NBA basketball player. And his conclusion is that everyone has the capacity to be a 'giant' in someone's eyes.

Just think about that in a workplace context for a second.

> **As a leader you have the ability to enthuse and motivate people, or completely irritate and piss them off in a heartbeat, with one careless word, tactless memo, or ill-advised tone.**

So if we're talking about value-for-money strategies for motivating people, driving performance and changing behaviour, make the most of your 'free words' – the return on investment can be priceless.

Sometimes, this means being a lighthouse; at other times you'll need to be the torch.

What do I mean by this? The lighthouse is the shining light beaming from the top of the cliffs, signalling the clear way forward to help others avoid foundering on the rocks.

The torch is required to make it down safely from those cliffs and take a more hands-on approach at ground level to the challenges at hand, rolling up your sleeves and leading by example.

Good leaders are able to switch seamlessly between the two, and have the ability to understand when, how and why to do it.

Part of this revolves around understanding your own brand. Who you are, who you are expected to be, and how you are perceived by the people that matter most.

> **As a leader, your brand is incredibly powerful and influential. The way you dress, the way you look, the way you speak, move, and interact with people.**

Your timekeeping, the vehicle you drive, the layout of your office, the tone of your communications, the way you chair meetings; it's all wrapped up in there.

Do you read the same books and journals as your colleagues do, or watch the same TV shows? Can you have a chat with them about the latest soap storylines, the weekend's big sports results, or new Hollywood film release? Do you eat in the staff canteen?

And if you're giving a speech, or taking to the stage to deliver a keynote address, what's your walk-on music of choice?

All of that has an impact on whether people think they can relate to you, and believe that you can understand the world in which they live, and the things in life that are important to them.

But how do you pinpoint what your brand actually is? How do you create it in the first place? And once you are up and running, can it be changed?

Those are not particularly easy questions to answer, but I can certainly tell you one thing – faking it is not the secret to making it.

Just be authentic. You'll get found out really quickly if you are not. Yes, you can refine your personality or smooth down some of your harder edges, but a sense of brand is not something that can be taught directly, downloaded from a self-help manual, or indeed built from scratch.

Someone came up to me on a training course the other day and said: "I hope you don't mind me stopping you to ask your advice, but you seem like an approachable person." A small incident in the grand scheme of things, but it was an incredibly rewarding and reassuring thing to hear.

(And no, before you ask, I didn't tell him to bugger off and leave me alone because I was too busy…!)

As I've already said, I'm no great poker player, but that doesn't mean I'm not interested in working out a particular person's 'tell'.

Micro expressions – momentary facial movements which can betray a person's anger, disgust, fear, happiness, sadness, or surprise – have always fascinated me. So have the nuances of body language.

> **I believe that knowing how to read a person's facial expressions is one of the most important people skills in business.**

For example, can you spot the difference between a fleeting look of anger or fear? Disgust or sadness? Surprise or delight?

All of these are betrayed in a micro expression, a brief, involuntary facial tell when a person experiences an emotion which is impossible to hide. They can come and go in the blink of an eye (which amusingly can be a tell itself too). Read them incorrectly, and it can be a recipe for trouble.

Micro expressions were first documented by researchers Haggard and Isaacs in the 1960s. Having said that, you can actually trace the theory as far back as Charles Darwin, who promoted the idea that people will express emotions in exactly the same way, whichever corner of the globe they call home.

Emotional psychologist Dr Paul Ekman then expanded the research to prove that the majority of micro expressions are universally recognised.

His work is the basis of the fabulous TV drama series Lie To Me, starring Tim Roth as the world's leading deception expert who studies facial expressions and involuntary body language to expose the truth behind the lies.

He teaches a course in body language and makes an honest fortune exploiting it, helping the police and various authorities to bring law breakers to justice. As the programme's tagline says: "He knows when you're lying."

If you're interested in the opportunities which mastering micro expressions can open up for you as a leader, it's well worth checking out.

> **One of the first things I do when I walk into a meeting room is to 'test the temperature' to get an early instinctive guide around what's in store, and to how things may pan out.**

In isolation, this is little more than a gut feeling which is meaningless, but if it's informed by being switched onto people's expressions and body language, it can be incredibly insightful.

Micro expressions are not to be confused with macro expressions or habits like body language. I cross my arms a lot, but that doesn't mean I'm disinterested. (Not necessarily, anyway!)

I look at all of these aspects as a suite of tools to build up a telling picture. If you are switched on to it all, you'll find you become much better at reading people and can sometimes use the information you are discreetly gathering to maybe move them subtly in the direction of travel you desire.

It's a fascinating science, which I feel is often under-exploited.

The pandemic brought a new aspect to all of this – online meeting etiquette.

There's a big difference between the way in-person meetings pan out, in comparison to sessions on platforms like Zoom or Teams.

In many ways, online calls have shifted the dynamics. People are much more prepared to shake their heads on a Zoom call because they are looking at a camera rather staring into someone's eyes.

I've found myself picking up on this a lot, and because it's quite a blunt tool, I've stopped meetings at times and confronted a person by saying to them: "I noticed you were shaking your head there - what's your opinion on this?'.

Leadership consultant Carol Kinsey Goman wrote an interesting piece for Forbes about how to read body language on Zoom, when the only thing you can see is their head.

She says there are still 15 body language signals that betray people's emotions and interests, such as a slight head tilt as a sign of engagement, and the speed of a nodding head – when someone nods slowly, she says it indicates an interest in whoever is speaking. A fast nod, though, can signal impatience.

And if people are feeling stressed or under pressure, Carol says you will often see people touching their faces – as well as blinking more frequently.

The message is clear: whatever form your meetings may take, don't underestimate the power of expression and body language to tell you much more than any words will express.

And remember, it works both ways....

"If you hire only those people you understand, the company will never get people better than you are. You often find outstanding people among those you don't particularly like."

Soichiro Honda, founder of Honda

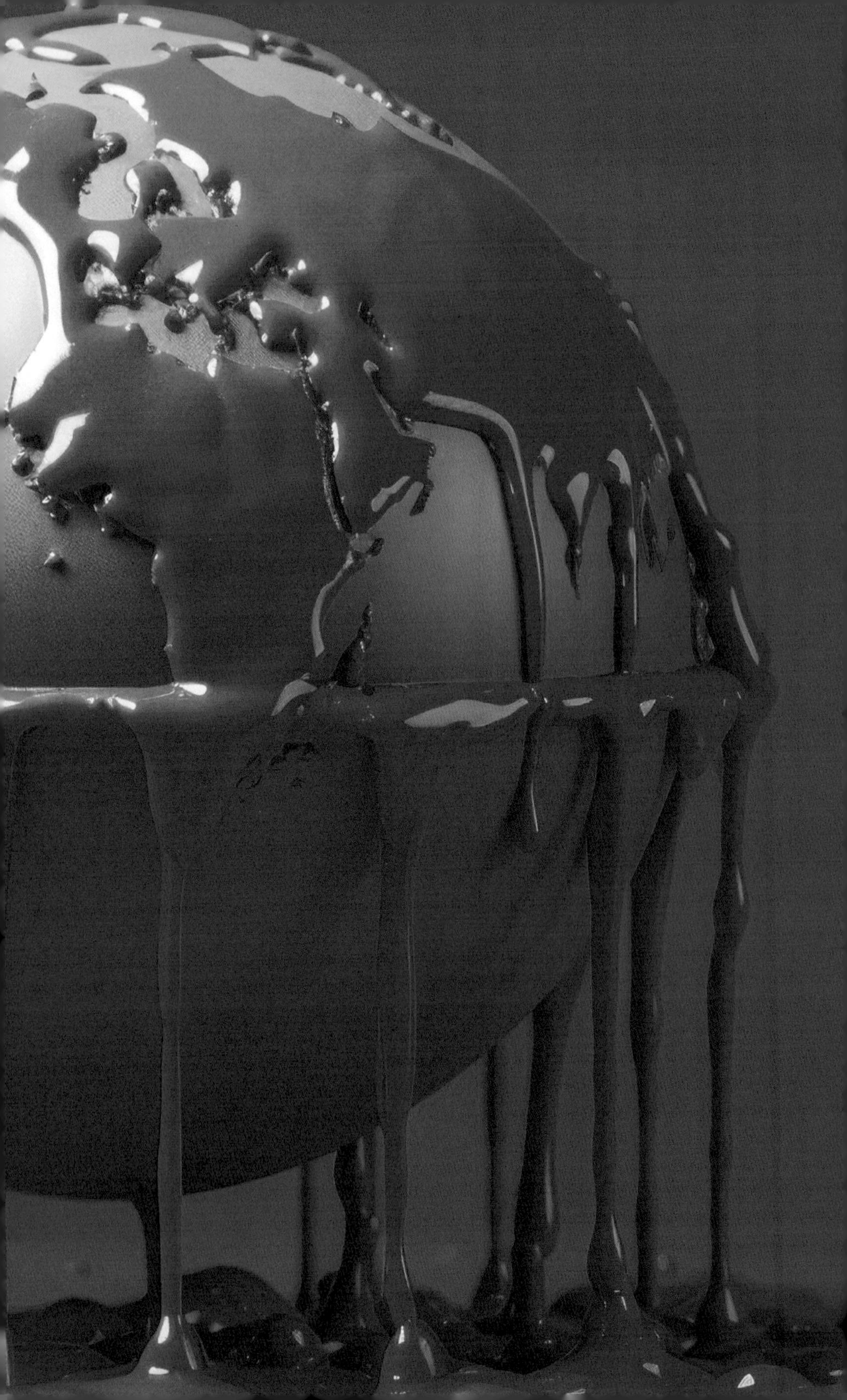

CHAPTER *thirteen*
Pre-mortem for a permacrisis

The Collins dictionary word of the year for 2022 was 'permacrisis'. It is officially described as an extended period of instability and insecurity, specifically resulting from a series of catastrophic events.

There's no doubting the fact that it captured that feeling that we were all lurching from one unprecedented world event to another at that time, and contemplating with a sense of trepidation what new horrors might be coming next.

Omnicrisis was another one – the feeling that everything was going to hell in a handcart at the same time.

Then there was its close cousin omnishambles, coined by the writers of political satire The Thick Of It for a situation which is shambolic from every possible angle. We've all experienced that environment at some stage, I'm sure.

> **Have you ever been in meetings when there's a decision which needs making and someone asks: "Well, what did we do last time?"**

Sometimes you will be faced with circumstances for which there has never been a 'last time' in our lifetimes, like the Covid pandemic for example.

And anyway, just because we did something last time won't mean it's the right strategy for now.

Whatever badge you give to these situations, though, one thing is for sure. Everyone likes to roll up their sleeves and make some noise when there's a crisis.

We saw this massively during Covid as people were happy to put their heads above the parapet to demonstrate how they were proactively working to dig us out of the mire.

The public sector are really good at it – although there's an argument (which they may not particularly thank me for making) that 99% of their work is actually entirely predictable.

What do I mean by this? Take social services as an example. Children grow up and become adults. Young adults grow up and become pensioners. And with all of this comes a very predictable set of challenges.

Yet somehow, when children come to transition to adulthood, there is always a flurry of last-minute activity – we always knew they were going to turn 18, so why does it often seem from behaviour patterns that this has come as a big surprise?

When you translate this into our work and take a moment to consider it, the vast majority of what we do is predictable. People don't always like to hear that, because they want to make their job look more dangerous, more edgy, more challenging perhaps.

There's something inside people that drives us to need to place ourselves in crisis mode, so we can pull on the fluorescent jackets and show our determination and stiff upper lip spirit.

But did we have to be there in the first place?

There's no doubting the fact that flipping into crisis mode gives you a rush of adrenaline, but these situations must always be the exception, not the norm. Otherwise you'll eventually keel over from what I describe as adrenal exhaustion.

Adrenaline is not designed to be a lifestyle choice; it's a short, sharp burst which is not meant to be sustainable. Overdose on it, and it's not going to be good for you.

It's a reference point to organisational fatigue as well. At work, people will naturally gravitate to doing the things they like, and leave the other stuff to one side.

There is a truth within this, so you have to understand what is demotivating about stuff you don't want to do, and recognise the aspects that appeal to you about the things you do want to do.

Clever leaders will work with this, do what they can to avoid having square pegs in round holes.

It's behavioural economics, and brings us back to this most important of points – how do you motivate people, drive people, and keep people happy and productive in their work? How do you remain aware of negative drivers that threaten this equilibrium?

Creating conditions for success is what it's all about.

You know the saying that if you enjoy what you do, you'll never work a day in your life. There's definitely something in that sentiment – you'll also be better at your job in most cases too if it's something you have a real passion for.

How do we create that passion? The leader has a pivotal role in this, through words, deeds and management styles.

It's about working on the conditions of the system to make them conditions for success. People don't always think enough about this.

Targets, management information, well-defined job roles, feedback processes, performance management, structure, IT support, regulation, reward, inspection . . . there are so many elements.

And recognising the balance between your team's willingness, and their wellbeing, is another important facet.

There is a lot of organisational fatigue around at the moment which means, in many cases, employees have less capacity to cope with major change.

Research has shown that an employee's ability to cope with change in their workplace is running at just 50% of pre-pandemic levels.

Why? Because so many staff have been 'running hot' for prolonged periods – it's back to that adrenaline issue again, which should be the exception, and not the norm.

We've spent so much time in crisis mode that there hasn't been an opportunity to recharge the batteries.

A business needs prosperity, but not at the expense of the wellbeing of its team. We have to find a balance.

And let us not forget that there is something for leaders to heed here too around our own wellbeing.

You're always told in the event on an in-air emergency that you should make sure your own oxygen mask is correctly applied before you set about helping others. This is really important.

It's a very British trait to view someone as being a fantastic asset to the team because they work 18 hours a day, sleep on a clothes line and are always on call.

Loyalty and commitment are two of the most important traits, but it doesn't have to look this way.

Everyone has to switch off and take a step away from their work station – to ensure that they can be brilliant when required.

But this underground culture, the unspoken 'expectation' that your job will be most secure if you are first in and last out of the office, is genuinely toxic.

The real evidence of a business culture is how we behave when no-one is watching.

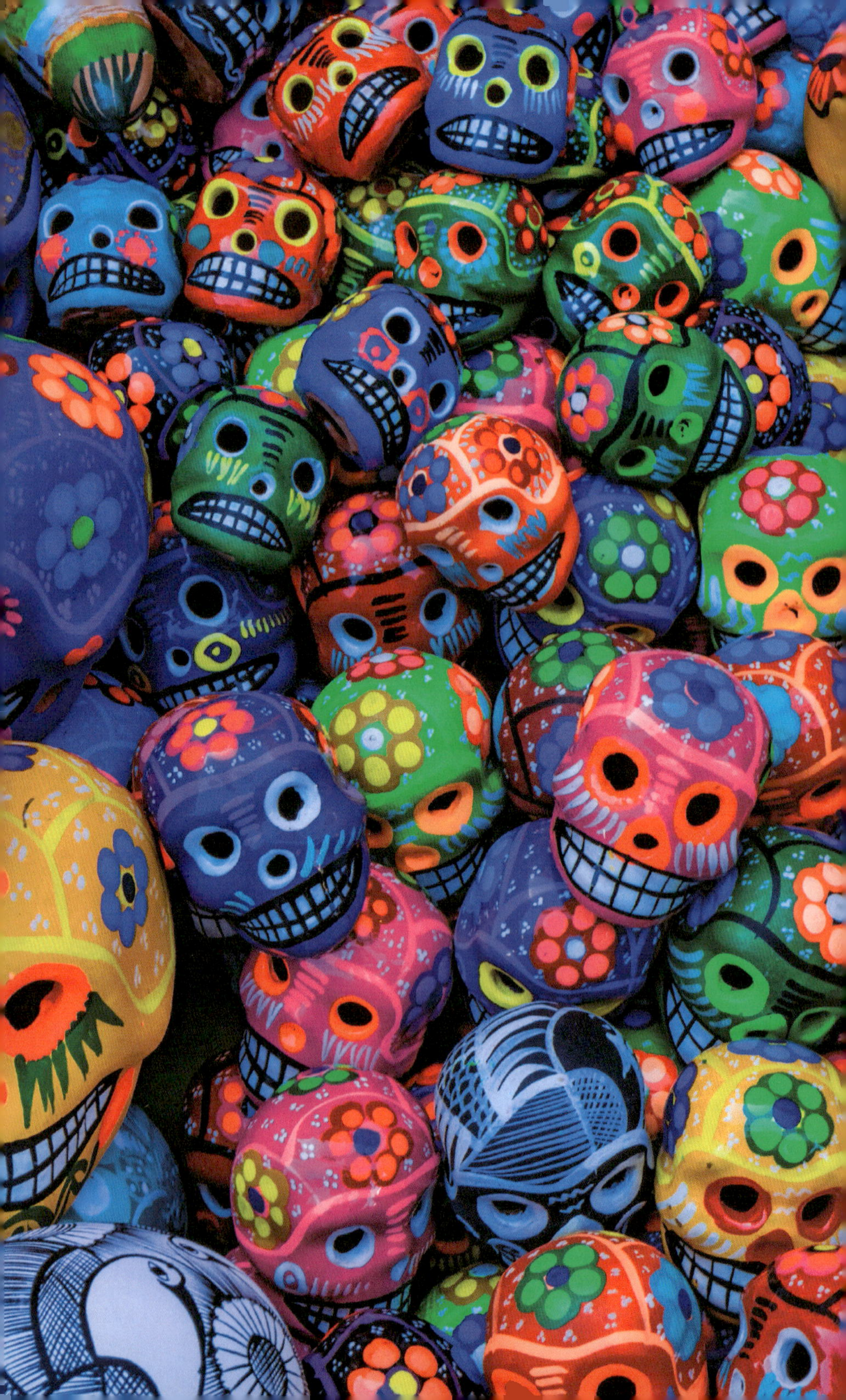

If an employee believes that their managers have their interests in mind, always consider the impact which change will have on the whole team, tell the truth and make good on their promises, chances are the culture will be healthy and productive.

It's sound practice to over-communicate with team members at times of change, and be as transparent as possible.

How many times do you hear customers bemoaning the 'lack of information' at airports or railway stations when transport systems are disrupted? It's almost always top of the list.

Staff who feel regularly updated will also feel most valued.

So much of our working lives are still built around Victorian cultures, and we seem incapable of weaning ourselves off them – even when common sense is screaming at us that it's the right thing to do.

Look at the controversy which the suggestion of switching to a four-day week created. Who says we have to have a two-day weekend? When was it agreed that the standard working day should be nine-to-five with an hour for lunch? And what makes you think that the rules of the 19th century are still relevant in the 21st, when virtually everything else around us has shifted beyond recognition?

I'll tell you why we don't change. It's because people fear being at the vanguard of a movement which may be judged differently when the benefit of good old hindsight is applied.

Sadly, it's stifling evolution and innovation. I think this is particularly prevalent in the public sector.

It's the classic 'risk v reward' dilemma. And yet the larger a risk an organisation is prepared to take, the greater the potential rewards will always be.

I am genuinely disappointed with the levels of ambition and innovation in many sectors of business – but few people are specifically rewarded for this aspect of their job, so the drivers are not there.

But the same applies to me. There is no financial bonus scheme linked to my style of thinking, but I believe it benefits the organisation in all sorts of different ways . . . and me, too.

And as a leader, if that's the kind of approach I'm demonstrating to colleagues, there is no excuse for them not to be that little bit braver themselves, that little bit more adventurous, and try to do the same.

And as I said, if 20% of decisions turn out to be wrong – I'm ok with that, as long as they were made on sound foundations. That's very different from them being bad.

Of course, you will always maximise your chances of a decision being the right one, with the power of foresight. I call it my pre-mortem strategy; thinking about things before they happen.

It belongs in the same school of thought as the T-Cup principle we discussed earlier, thinking clearly under pressure.

A good manager will predict and dissect every scenario that could happen at any moment in time, and understand what needs to be done in every case. Before it happens.

Forgive me for another sporting analogy, but it's a perfect illustration here. Imagine you're all square in the World Cup final with a minute to go – what's your strategy for scoring the winner? If you've practised it time and time again, you're going to have the clarity of thought that's required.

Remember that famous Jonny Wilkinson drop goal in the dying moments of the 2003 Rugby World Cup? He knew precisely what to do in that split second, and executed it coolly and clinically under the most intense pressure.

> **Pre-mortem planning is about considering all the potential variations ahead of time, and coming up with a strategy for each and every one of them.**

In the event of one of the situations materialising, it gives you an enormous sense of confidence, reassurance and security . . . coupled with the strategies we've already outlined about absorbing uncertainty. This genuinely has been a game-changer for me and served me well in the face of ambiguity and volatility

Sometimes it involves trying to overlay some predictable aspects of what is unpredictable by definition. You work through those scenarios, and the more you think about it, the clearer your thinking in times of pressure is likely to be.

Emergency planning officers are a good example here. Their entire job description is to plan for an unforeseen situation, which sounds like a contradiction.

But the principles are the same. Sometimes you have to prepare to crash; think that the worst could happen to your business, and have a calmly crafted plan for what you would do about it.

It removes a lot of the stress if you have already mapped out a way forward, and you're far less likely to fall foul of adrenal exhaustion.

You'll be able to de-stress because you know the steps. That's the beauty of a pre-mortem – you won't know the timing, but you'll know precisely what your action plan is to the finest of points, understand how to put it into practice, and be aware of the likely consequences.

It de-pressurises what can be very difficult and dangerous situations where decision-makers might otherwise lose their heads.

"If you have that energy in you that you really want to make something creative and make something that's going to impact the world, then go for it, do it and don't let anybody tell you no."

John Legend

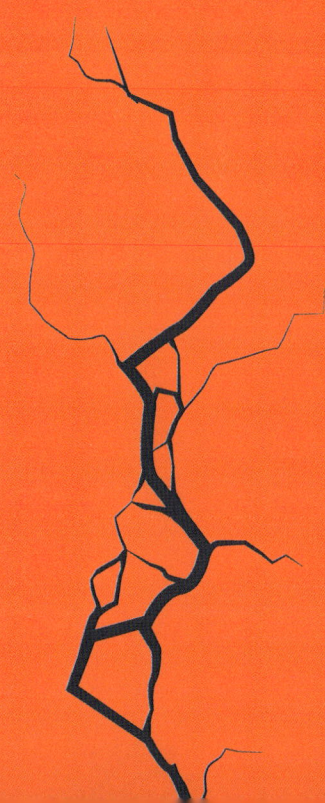

CHAPTER *fourteen*
Success(ion)

No-one was born a leader, manager, or chief executive; people grow into these positions. And one thing is for certain – the journey is neither simple, nor linear.

It will have been emotional at times, and frustrating at others. It will have been rewarding, ugly, funny, fantastic, depressing, exciting, disappointing, perplexing, challenging, and amazing.

Along the way it will have meant learning to come to terms with the harsh fact that you are not always going to be right, and can never be universally popular.

I'm well aware that what I've been writing about here isn't going to be everyone's cup of tea. Not everyone will consider my ideas relevant to their career development or personal or professional development – in fact I may have proffered theories and trains of thought which you fundamentally take issue with.

And that's absolutely OK.

Hopefully, though, the fact that you've made it this far signals that you are finding some useful information or tools which bring fresh perspective to the art of leadership, management and problem solving, encouraging you to approach problems and challenges in a different, or indeed multi-faceted way. Removing the blinkers.

If that's the case, then I feel my work here is nearly done. Nearly, but not quite...

There's still time for some music. What sort of music, you ask? Well that's entirely up to you.

The visceral emotions you feel when you hear a particularly moving piece of music are like no other. It releases something in our brains called dopamine, which has the power to trigger sensations of pleasure and a feeling of being blissfully happy with the world.

Gradually, as your brain starts to become more familiar with a particular tune, you'll get that kick of happy drug just by hearing the first few notes. It's why we all have perennial favourites on our playlists.

So let me ask you this; have you ever considered putting some music on in the background when you are at the office? Many people have, and do it every day. But if not, why not? And more importantly, what's stopping you?

Is it the thought that for every thrash metal fan in the room there will be another who prefers the soothing tones of Michael Buble, and it'll cause a bitter row over the playlist? Or is it – as I'll venture to suggest in many cases – more likely that it's just never occurred to you as being an appropriate or relevant thing to do?

Visit your local law firm, your accountant or the local council offices and the chances of hearing music playing in the background as people go about their work are pretty remote.

Walk into a graphic design agency, a marketing hub, or a distribution warehouse on the other hand and there is highly likely to be some music playing not far away.

So ask yourself, are you missing a trick here? Are there significant benefits to be had by throwing something of a curve ball into your work environment and doing something that people simply wouldn't expect?

Tactically, it could open the doors to . . . well, who knows what in your business.

It could set you apart as a progressive, shrugging aside those outdated operating paradigms which discourage us from opening our eyes to possibilities, and discourage us from being consistently curious.

The simple act of a colleague wandering through the room and saying: "What's with the music playing in the background?" could be the opening salvo of an interaction which may bond work colleagues on a different level to anything that has gone before.

And that's without even getting into the wider debate about the psychological impact you could be making. There are medical journals which purport to have evidence that listening to soothing and gentle music in the office can reduce stress levels and negative feelings, and I can believe it.

Our connection to music matters to us more than we know, and yet we are really limited in thinking around this in a business environment.

There are some fairly cheap and swift things you can do to change the working environment and atmosphere when required, and making use of music is most definitely one of them.

If you've ever given a keynote speech, or been the master of ceremonies at a public event, chances are you will have been asked by the production crew if you have a preference for your walk-on music.

It had probably never occurred to you before that point. And yet it will be more of a talking point than you could ever have imagined; it will have had more longevity, quite probably, than anything you had to say once you reached the microphone. I remember someone stopping me at a particular event and saying 'any chief exec that walks on to AC/DC gets my vote!' Music is a trigger.

Not convinced? More than a quarter of a century on, can you remember anything Tony Blair had to say when he gave his victory speech after winning the 1997 general election? Almost certainly not, but I bet you remember that he walked on to the sound of 'Things Can Only Get Better'.

On the opposite side of the political divide, we also remember Theresa May opting for Dancing Queen ahead of her conference speech – for slightly less flattering reasons!

But that's the point. Good or bad, hilarious or provocative, music is a window into our personalities.

We are all multi-faceted humans capable of communicating with sound, light, taste, touch . . . let's use them all.

Have you ever stopped to think about how you'll be remembered, or what your epitaph might be?

I have a phrase which I often say to people: create your own shadow, because you can't control anyone else's.

It goes back to what we were discussing earlier around issues of imposter syndrome, and feeling worthy of the position you hold.

Personally, I'm not the least bit motivated by a desire to leave my own footprint in the business world. I know many that are – and many that shouldn't be.

I'm more concerned with living in the present, and following my principles of co-operation, collaboration and reciprocity.

You should plough your own furrow, and worry more about what's important to you as an individual than about how you may look in the eyes of others.

> **Authenticity, I believe, is the secret to being assured, astute, and ambitious.**

It speaks to the core of what much of this book explores. If you pause too often to consider the liabilities and consequences of your job, you'll be having sleepless nights, and find yourself paralysed by fear. You have to keep focused on the road ahead.

So much of what you encounter at leadership level will be out of your control, so what's the point in stressing about it?

Happiness is so important in our working lives. The bottom line for me is that I do a job because I enjoy it. I find humour in my day-to-day dealings as much as I find frustration.

You should never lose sight of the characteristics of your job which make you want to get out of bed in the morning.

So often I hear of people who embark on their so-called dream career only to find that as they progress through the ranks, fewer and fewer elements of the job that they really enjoyed remain part of their brief.

If you recognise yourself in that, maybe it's time to be honest with yourself; to ask yourself some tough questions. To consider if you've made a wrong decision – not, as we said earlier, a bad decision, because it could have seemed right for you at the time.

There's nothing weak about admitting you've done something wrong.

Truth be told, none of us know what's really around the corner, do we? Few of us can legitimately claim to have a grasp on what Artificial Intelligence has the capacity to do to our world in the years to come. At the moment, it's a battle between technology-led efficiency, and the preservation of personality.

Just a few years ago it would have been unimaginable to see companies proudly advertising that you will speak to a 'real person' if you call their switchboard. It was just taken for granted.

Now, it's seen almost as a USP. To continue the musical thread, we've got vinyl coming back as well – largely, I believe, because of the 'personality' which it gives to an artist in comparison with a soulless streaming service.

What's my point here? That we don't ever want to live in a cloned world. We need to create sceptics, and avoid at all costs simply surrounding ourselves with mini-me characters.

A degree of scepticism is healthy in everyone. We should never take what we are told on face value. We should be curious.

It's the pathway to a healthy debate. If you can find common ground with the most vocal of sceptics, more often than not you'll find they turn out to be your most trusted and solid advocates.

There will always be those who cross the line, of course, who work really hard at being challenging all of the time.

If they applied half that energy actually doing their job, they'd be brilliant. In leadership, you encounter the full spectrum.

The art is to remain genuinely curious about how best to connect with people, and to know when the time has come to cut your losses and give up.

> **Relational intelligence – the ability to recognise and understand the emotions, values and interests of yourself and others – is just as important as rational intelligence.**

Sometimes, being curious means commissioning the problem, not the solution.

What do I mean by this? When people are looking to commission a service, or buy a product, their first instinct is to go out and simply buy whatever best fit the market has to offer, or negotiate on the basis of a set menu which is presented to them.

I prefer a different way of looking at this. Why be constrained? Why not ignore what's being offered to you out there and simply go to the market with a simple question: "I'm trying to solve this particular problem. Can you help?"

Now you might well end up in the same place with a solution that was sitting on the shelf all along.

But what if that question leads to something bespoke, something exciting, something unique? Wouldn't that be so much more rewarding, impactful – and fun? If you don't try it, you'll never know.

As Albert Einstein said: "Without changing our pattern of thought, we will not be able to solve the problems we created with our current patterns of thought."

So how are you feeling right now? Basking in a newly-discovered motivational clarity, mired in managerial befuddlement, or just suffering from a nasty dose of 'so what?' syndrome?

Me? Through the process of writing this book, I've found myself contemplating whether I'm a scholar of leadership ideals, or whether I simply want to absorb and learn for the purpose of developing my career.

What comes first, the academic, or the business person? It's an interesting and quite complex debate.

I think that academia provides you with a framework, but what I'm really looking for in this life is to capitalise on any opportunities to gain an advantage. That's what personal development is. And that's the inquisitive business person in me.

Pioneering thinker Russell Ackoff describes himself as the founding member of the Presentology Society for people who concern themselves with the here and now. I'm a devoted member of that fraternity.

Like him, I have no interest whatsoever in reconstructing the past as I would have liked to see it.

You don't learn from sitting still and reading historical documents about other people's mistakes. You learn from making your own, and should never be penalised or discouraged from doing so.

Don't just engage with the next shiny big thing to go viral on social media.

Don't take advice from people who refuse to observe and analyse the changing world around them.

Don't chase someone else's future.

Create, nurture, recognise and celebrate your own personal milestones and achievements.

I didn't row the Atlantic
#so*what*

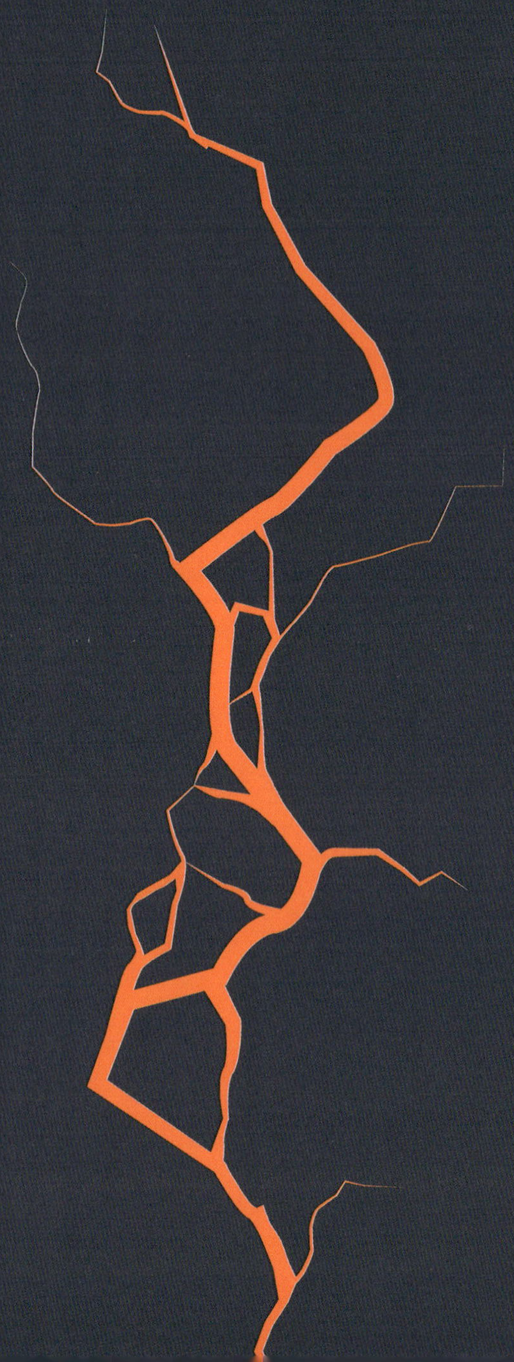

Acknowledgements

As I mentioned right at the beginning of this journey, there's absolutely nothing wrong with soaking up snippets of wisdom from others.

Why re-invent the wheel if someone has created a perfectly operational tool already?

This is why I've made no apology for adding context to my thoughts by quoting wise words of wisdom from a diverse array of sources.

It's only right and proper to give them the acknowledgement they merit for this, so I say thank you, in no particular order, for the minds and the methodologies of:

- Scott Adams
- John Amaechi
- Dan Ariely
- Alex Bellos
- Roy T Bennett
- Dale Carnegie
- Peter Drucker
- Stephen Dubner
- Amy Edmondson
- Darren Edwards
- Dr Paul Ekman
- Carol Kinsey Goman
- Ernest Hemingway
- Soichiro Honda
- Damian Hughes
- William James
- Steve Jobs
- Carl Jung
- James Kerr
- Hugh Mackay
- Paul McGee
- Tim Minchin
- Vilfredo Pareto
- Nirmal 'Nims' Purja
- Chris Rose
- Nick Sanders
- Sir Clive Woodward
- Master Fuchan Yuan

Editorial consultant: Carl Jones
Design: Michelle Dalton
Adobe pictures published under licence.
All Blacks rugby picture: James Coleman

Printed in Great Britain
by Amazon